THE FUTURE OF
GAS AND OIL
FROM THE SEA

THE FUTURE OF GAS AND OIL FROM THE SEA

Edited by

GERARD J. MANGONE

VNR VAN NOSTRAND REINHOLD COMPANY
NEW YORK CINCINNATI TORONTO LONDON MELBOURNE

Copyright © 1983 by Van Nostrand Reinhold Company Inc.

Library of Congress Catalog Card Number: 82-11010
ISBN: 0-442-26164-0

Manufactured in the United States of America

Published by Van Nostrand Reinhold Company Inc.
135 West 50th Street, New York, N.Y. 10020

Van Nostrand Reinhold Publishing
1410 Birchmount Road
Scarborough, Ontario M1P 2E7, Canada

Van Nostrand Reinhold
480 Latrobe Street
Melbourne, Victoria 3000, Australia

Van Nostrand Reinhold Company Limited
Molly Millars Lane
Wokingham, Berkshire, England

15 14 13 12 11 10 9 8 7 6 5 4 3 2 1

Library of Congress Cataloging in Publication Data

The Future of gas and oil from the sea.
   Includes index.
   1. Petroleum in submerged lands. 2. Gas, Natural,
in submerged lands. I. Mangone, Gerard J.
TN871.3.F87   1983   333.8'23   82-11010
ISBN: 0-442-26164-0

Contributors

Gerard J. Mangone is H. Rodney Sharp Professor of International Law and Organization, and Director of the Center for the Study of Marine Policy at the University of Delaware. He received his Ph.D. in international law at Harvard University, and he has been a professor or visiting professor at Wesleyan, Mt. Holyoke, Yale, Swarthmore, Princeton, Syracuse, and Johns Hopkins University. He was appointed as the Tagore Law Professor at Calcutta University, India.

Dr. Mangone has also been Dean, Vice President, and Provost at Temple University, the first Senior Fellow of the Woodrow Wilson International Center for Scholars, and the Executive Director of the President's Commission on the United Nations in Washington. He is the single author of nine books, the coauthor of nineteen other books, and the editor of eleven books, as well as the editor of the annual *Marine Policy Reports*. Dr. Mangone has traveled abroad on research assignments every year for thirty-three consecutive years.

Pierre Samuel duPont IV received his Bachelor of Science degree in mechanical engineering from Princeton University in 1956, and his Bachelor of Law degree from Harvard University Law School in 1963. From 1969–71, he served in the Delaware House of Representatives; from 1971–77, he served as a member of the U.S. House of Representatives; and in 1977, he was elected Governor of the State of Delaware, and reelected in 1980. Governor duPont has served as Chairman of the Committee on Community and Economic Development of the National Governor's Association; on the Executive Committee of the Council of State Governments; and as Vice Chairman of the Southern Governor's Conference.

Edgar S. Driver is General Manager of Exploration Research for Gulf Science and Technology Company, Pittsburgh, PA. He received his B.A. in mathematics from Dartmouth College (1943), an M.S. in mathematics from University of Pittsburgh (1959). His Gulf career began as a geophysicist at the Gulf Research Center (1945), progressed through research and operational positions including Chief Geophysicist for Mene Grande Oil Company (Venezuela), and Manager of Gulf's Marine Exploration Program which developed the R/V GULFREX as the industry's first multisensor geophysical research vessel having full onboard processing and interpretation. He served on panels of International Program of Ocean Drilling and National Research Council. In 1945 he was awarded Order of British Empire membership for service to British 8th Army (Africa and Europe).

Barclay P. Collins is a Supervisor in the Seismic Evaluation Section, Gulf Science and Technology Company in Pittsburgh, PA. He received a B.S. in physics from the College of William and Mary, and his M.S. and Ph.D. in marine geology from the Graduate School of Oceanography, University of Rhode Island. Since joining Gulf Science and Technology Company in 1978 he has been involved with interpretation of geophysical data, analysis of frontier basins, and acquisition and interpretative processing of seismic data.

Herbert Skolnick is Senior Administrative Associate on the staff of the General Manager for Exploration Research, Gulf Science and Technology Company, Pittsburgh, PA. He received his B.S. degree from Brooklyn College (1947), his M.S. degree from the University of Oklahoma (1949), and his Ph.D. from the University of Iowa (1952). He joined Gulf in 1952 and has served in a variety of exploration and research capacities for Gulf in the United States, the Canary Islands, and West Africa.

N. Terrance Edgar, born in Bristol, England in 1933, received his B.A. at Middlebury College in Vermont, his M.S. at Florida State University, and he received his Ph.D. in 1968 at Columbia University in New York City. He is currently the Chief, Office of Marine Geology at the U.S. Geological Survey in Reston, Virginia. His prior major assignments were as a field geologist with Shell Oil Company of Canada; working in marine seismic refraction and reflection as a graduate student in geophysics with the Lamont-Doherty Geological Observatory; and as Chief Scientist, Deep Sea Drilling Project at the Scripps Institution of Oceanography until December 1975, immediately prior to his present assignment with the USGS. Dr. Edgar has been a fellow of the Geological Society of America for 13 years and has been a member of the American Association for the Advancement of Science since 1966.

J. Preston Mason is president of Seaflo Systems, Inc. in Houston, Texas, an engineering company specializing in the application of seafloor wells and floating production systems. He has a M.S. degree in chemical engineering from Northwestern University. During the past fifteen years, Mr. Mason has been actively involved in development and application of production systems for hydrocarbon reserves located in deep water and hostile environments. Prior to forming SEAFLO in 1978, Mr. Mason was with Exxon. He participated in developing Exxon's Subsea Production System (SPS) and eventually supervised the subsea research group for that organization. Mr. Mason is a registered professional engineer in Texas and a member of several engineering societies.

Hans Jahns is a research scientist with Exxon Production Research Company, Houston, Texas. Born in Germany, he attended the Technical University at Clausthal, Germany, where he received diploma degrees in geology and in mining engineering, and a doctorate in petroleum engineering. He began his professional career in 1959 with Wintershall AG, in Nienhagen near Celle, Germany, and joined Exxon in 1962 as a research engineer at Jersey Production

Research Company in Tulsa, Oklahoma. With Exxon, he has worked in several fields, including reservoir engineering, reservoir description, oceanography, and arctic engineering, and he has played a leading role in Exxon's Arctic research efforts since 1968. He became a member of the National Research Council's Committee on Permafrost in 1977 and is currently serving on the Council's Polar Research Board.

Don Lambert, editor of *Pipe Line Industry,* has devoted more than 26 years of his professional life to petroleum industry journalism. He received his Bachelor of Journalism degree from the University of Missouri in 1950, and worked on his Masters at Northwestern University. He held editorial and executive positions with the United States Junior Chamber of Commerce and had several year's petroleum industry experience with Standard Oil Company of New Jersey before joining Gulf Publishing Company as managing editor for three magazines in 1955. He was promoted to associate editor of *Pipe Line Industry* and *World Oil* magazines in 1958, and was named editor of *Pipe Line Industry* in 1969. His in-depth reports in Gulf Publishing magazines have won five national awards for editorial achievement. He was presented the 1980 Pipeliner of the Year Award for "outstanding contributions to pipelining."

Roland E. Bulow is supervisor, Marine Research and Testing, for Mobil Shipping and Transportation Company. He received his Bachelor of Engineering (mechanical) degree from City College, New York, and is a licensed professional engineer (N.Y. State). He was project engineer for development of the first two tankers for offshore loading in the Beryl Field in the North Sea, and was task force leader for the "Statfjord Unit Offshore Loading Study," prepared for the Norwegian government. He coauthored and presented a paper entitled "Offshore Storage and Loading," for the Offshore North Sea Technology Conference in Stavanger, Norway, in 1978.

Scott G. Withee is a senior project engineer in the Marine Research Department of Mobil Shipping & Transportation Company. He has a Bachelor of Science Degree in naval architecture and marine engineering from Webb Institute of Naval Architecture, and a Masters Degree in business administration (finance) from Adelphi University. He was involved in the preparation of the Statfjord Offshore Loading Study and has been involved in motions and transportation efficiency analyses of both the Beryl and Statfjord ALP's.

Thomas S. McIntosh is president of Zapata Off-Shore Company, an international offshore drilling contractor, which operates a fleet of 20 drilling rigs worldwide. McIntosh received a B.S. degree in mechanical engineering from Rice University, and an M.B.A. from Stanford. Before becoming president of Zapata Off-Shore, he served as ZOS' Vice President for Marketing, and as Vice President of Corporate Development for ZOS' parent firm, Zapata Corporation. McIntosh is active in trade and professional organizations, having served as president of the International Association of Drilling Contractors during 1980.

Lawrence R. Zeitlin is professor of industrial psychology and director of the Human Factors Laboratory at the City University of New York. Concurrently he is president of Lakeview Research, Inc., a consulting firm specializing in maritime and industrial personnel and safety problems.

Trained as both a physicist (Harvard, 1951) and a social scientist (Northwestern, 1954), Dr. Zeitlin has explored the man-machine interaction for most of his career. In the mid-50s he served in the U.S. Army (Army Medical Research Laboratory) directing cold weather man-machine research in support of an Arctic Circle combat potential. During the next decade he held senior research and management positions with RCA Airborne Systems, Bendix Systems, Dunlap and Associates, and Bell Laboratories. He was actively involved in the Polaris program and the manned space flight program.

He was appointed to the CUNY Doctoral Faculty in 1964 to organize a graduate program in Industrial Psychology. In 1974 he started Lakeview Research, Inc. to conduct sociotechnical research for the maritime industry.

Thomas McCloskey received a B.A. from Notre Dame and a Masters Degree from the Monterey Institute of Foreign Studies. He was a special assistant to the Assistant Secretary for Energy and Minerals, U.S. Department of the Interior. His primary responsibility was to oversee the preparation and publication of regulations governing the activities of oil and gas companies on the outer continental shelf. Besides giving overall policy guidance, he served as the intermediary between the Office of Energy and Minerals and the offices of the other Assistant Secretaries, Solicitor, and U.S. Geological Survey to resolve conflicts and gain consensus on five separate regulatory packages. Mr. McCloskey also served, for seven years, as the executive director of the Citizens Advisory Council to the Pennsylvania Department of Environmental Resources, which required familiarity with environmental issues and expertise in the internal workings of a highly technical, state government agency. He is a principal partner in Hooks, McCloskey & Associates. Since forming the firm, he has provided advice and services on regulatory and environmental matters in the areas of offshore and onshore mineral resource development and coastal zone management.

Dale Straughan is a Senior Research Scientist at the Institute for Marine and Coastal Studies at the University of Southern California. She received her Ph.D. in Zoology at the University of Queensland, Australia in 1966. She then worked at the James Cooke University in Australia and Hawaii Institute of Marine Biology before becoming associated with the Allan Hancock Foundation at the University of Southern California. She has conducted research on the impact of large oil spills (e.g., Santa Barbara and *Metula*) as well as long term chronic exposure to petroleum in the marine environment for a number of national and international organizations, and has authored over 100 articles.

Preface

In 1982 there was a glut of oil on the world market. The energy "crisis" of the previous years seemed to have been almost forgotten in the headlines about economic recession in the United States and battles in Asia, the Middle East, and South America. The employment of drilling rigs to search for gas and oil was declining while investments in non-conventional energy sources faltered. There was a surplus of tankers to carry the slow demand for crude oil while the production of gasoline and heating oil at refineries levelled off.

History teaches how rapidly unforeseen events can change the direction of society. But it is certain that any expanding economy needs energy from one source or another. In the near term in the modern world, neither coal, water pressure, nuclear power, nor rays from the sun are likely to displace the central role of gas and oil in providing immediate, clean, comparatively inexpensive sources of energy, especially as fuels in the special demands for civil transportation and military machines. But gas and oil are non-renewable resources that are slowly being depleted. Economic incentives and technological improvements, nevertheless, have enabled geologists and engineers to find and recover hydrocarbons from new places or new depths, on land and under the sea, which have prolonged the utility of this source of energy for the benefit of world society.

With this premise it seemed most timely and appropriate for the Center for the Study of Marine Policy at the University of Delaware to convene a national conference on the future of gas and oil from the sea in order to examine the location and extent of hydrocarbon resources in submerged lands, particularly in the basins or reservoirs of the continental shelf adjacent to the United States, and to analyze the methods by which those resources might be most efficiently, economically, and safely produced.

For the planning and implementation of the conference I had the benefit of the advice of Rex Alford, James Curlin, V. C. Eisler, John C. Estes, Adrian S. Hooper, Dobie Langenkamp, Griff C. Lee, Charles

D. Matthews, T. S. McIntosh, and especially S. J. Reso. Moreover, the following agencies and firms generously contributed to the support of the conference: Bethlehem Steel, Conoco, Exxon, Gulf Oil, Interstate and Ocean Transport, Phillips Petroleum, Texaco, the UNIDEL Foundation, Union Oil of California, and the U.S. Department of Energy.

Let it be clear for the record that none of the above is responsible for facts or opinions as expressed in this book by the several authors and edited at the Center for the Study of Marine Policy.

Others who made significant contributions to the conference were Hollis Hedberg, Ronald L. Geer, Admiral John B. Hayes, Hal Scott, Al Powers, Robert H. Lawton, Charles E. Walker, Congressman Edwin B. Forsythe, Senator Lowell P. Weicker, and John Bryne, to whom I am grateful.

I would like to express my appreciation to Maxwell S. McKnight, who represents the Center in Washington, to Susan Scotto, Porter Hoagland III, and Neal Shapiro, for their part in organizing and administering the conference, and to Mary Duricek, our executive secretary, who painstakingly processed the edited and re-edited copies of the entire manuscript.

From the text it will be seen that as much gas and oil remains to be found under the world ocean as already has been found under dry land. The challenge to drill and recover hydrocarbon resources from frontier areas, under deep water roiled by high winds or in frigid Arctic areas, has been described by the authors with illustrations of the advancing technology in drilling rigs and their equipment, new types of tankers and vessel transfers, and improved pipeline transmission of gas and oil. Moreover, the human factor of training and safety, critical to the efficient use of modern technology, have been explored. The book also examines the effect of regulation of the offshore industry by the government through the Outer Continental Shelf Act and its administration as well as the problems of ascertaining the environmental effects of the recovery of gas and oil from the seabed.

Whatever the economic climate of 1983 and 1984, there is a bright future for the recovery of gas and oil from the sea. Better geological knowledge and engineering skills will enable us to cope with hostile environments and to provide transport facilities that will expertly link the sources of supply with the areas of demand. More experience with the environmental effects of the offshore industry upon marine fisheries and coastline amenities should provide faster and more rational decisions in public regulation to obtain resources at minimal cost under proper environmental safeguards. It is the hope of the Center for the Study of Marine Policy that this book will provide expert data from the offshore gas and oil industry, clarify past experience and future developments in the recovery of hydrocarbons from submerged areas, and suggest the options for sound public policy decisions to maintain a reliable energy supply.

GERARD J. MANGONE
Director

Newark, Delaware

Foreword
The Crisis in American Government

Pierre S. duPont

We in the United States have lived through troubled times during the past two decades. If the decade of the sixties brought forth a crisis in our social and foreign policies, the decade of the seventies was, in a very real sense, a crisis in our economic policies. The results of the so-called American economic malaise through the 1970s are well known and documented: declining rates of growth, increasing levels of unemployment, the evolution of our foreign energy dependence, the decline of our dollar, and soaring rates of inflation, all of which have become commonplace in our daily lives.

It seems clear that what we face is not a crisis in American capitalism, not a crisis in American business or American productivity; rather what we are facing in the United States is the result of a crisis in government policy.

Increasingly burdensome taxes, unprecedented governmental deficits, misguided energy policies, tax policies that discourage investment while encouraging consumption and borrowing, oppressive and expanding governmental regulations, and, most importantly, run-away inflation made possible by an overly expansive monetary policy have all combined to sap our economic strength, to reduce our rates of growth, to increase our levels of unemployment, to weaken our dollar, to threaten our foreign policy, and even to make us doubt ourselves and our future.

But just as the tortured economic record of the 1970s was the predictable result of our misguided governmental policies, so too can the economic promise for the 1980s be turned around by a shift in the fundamental economic policies of our government. If we learn from the mistakes of the 1970s, the 1980s can indeed be a time of economic revitalization, increasing rates of growth, declining levels of unemployment and inflation, and a better standard of living for all of our citizens.

Perhaps the best example of the crisis of government policy during the 1970s was in energy. It was often said that Washington had no energy policy in the mid-seventies. In the words of one government official, it was a policy that encouraged consumption and discouraged production. It placed the greatest demand on fuels that were in the most scarce supply (oil and natural gas) while discouraging consumption of the more plentiful forms of energy (coal and nuclear). And, to make up for the resultant fuel shortages, that policy relied upon foreign imports of oil.

The flawed national energy policy of the 1970s was costing U.S. industry $500 million a year to administer and the federal government $200 million per year to enforce. It caused long lines of cars waiting for gasoline in the cities and towns of the United States. It sapped our nation's economic vitality, it inflated our economy, it undermined the value of our dollar, and it put thousands of people out of work.

In short, the failure to enact a sensible energy program disrupted our economy, pitted American against American, and yet failed to deliver a single additional Btu of energy to the American people.

The question has never been whether alternative energy sources could meet our needs. The question, rather, surrounds the price necessary to develop these alternative sources and the time required to bring them on stream. What price must be paid, both for the direct and the indirect costs, to develop our energy resources? In addition to production costs, there will be environmental costs that must figure in the price. Moreover, higher costs will be required to overcome the difficulties of transportation and temporary dislocations of plant, equipment, and personnel. But the central fact is that the world does have sufficient energy, *if* — and that's a big "if" — if it is willing to pay the price necessary to tap the potential.

Much of our policy in the 1970s accepted the idea, almost unchallenged, that energy controls were necessary because of the hardships and inequities that the free market pricing of energy cause. This assumed, first of all, that by controlling the price of domestic crude oil for example, the price of gasoline and heating oil would be maintained. We saw the flaw of that logic. But even more damaging to the dogma of fixing prices, it is not at all clear that effective controls will really improve fairness or reduce inequities. On the contrary, controls often do little other than artificially shift the inequities from one group to another and increase the total price paid.

It is the poor and the disadvantaged who get laid off first in a weak economy, who pay the highest costs when they can't get gasoline, and who have few alternatives when heating oil runs out. To suggest that, in the name of social fairness, the United States was better served by an energy controls policy that inflated our money, dislocated our workers, weakened our dollar abroad, undermined our national defense, increased consumption, inhibited productivity, and caused widespread personal frustration seems to tally unrealistic.

Instead of learning the hard lesson from the oil control program of the 1970s, we persisted in a natural gas policy that defied human understanding and could have continued controls until 1987 and beyond. Surely the people and industries of the United States would rather have adequate supplies of natural gas at the market price than no gas at a controlled price.

The 1970s was also the era of the "super deficit" as well as the decade of the energy mess. Except for the $25 million deficit in 1968 at the height of the Viet Nam Intervention, U.S. budget deficits had never risen to double digit percentages except in war time. The federal deficit soared to $66 million in 1976 and thereafter did not drop below $28 billion annually even during the economic upsurge of 1977–1978. The balanced budget of 1981 predicted by President Jimmy Carter was headed for a deficit of nearly $60 billion, and the policies of President Ronald Reagan to cut federal expenses will still leave a substantial gap between the government's income and outgo.

In addition to the unprecedented budget deficits, tax burdens also began to rise precipitously in the latter part of the 1970s. The increasing tax burdens on all Americans have had, in the judgment of many, an unfortunate, but predictable, negative impact on savings, on investment, and on the level of total output. And while the government tax and fiscal policies spun out of control, its regulatory policies burdened industry and the consumers with increasing costs. The Center for the Study of American Business at Washington University in St. Louis estimated the cost of government regulations in 1980 at $90 billion for American industry, which largely passed into prices for the American people.

But of all the government policies that contributed to American economic decline during the 1970s, none was more catastrophic than the government's failure to control inflation. The 1970s brought unprecedented rates of inflation to the American economy. More than any other single factor it caused the social problems of the 1970s. The inflation rate at the beginning of the decade was about five or six percent. By the end of the decade it was vacillating between ten and fifteen percent.

The 1970s began with a view expressed by many, such as Professor James Tobin of Yale University, then dean of Keynesian economists, that inflation was the least difficult and most politically acceptable method of allocating limited national resources to almost unlimited national demands. Essentially a lax monetary policy and an expansive fiscal policy allowed politicians to avoid making difficult but responsible political choices.

To illustrate the faulty economic policy of the United States, compare the Washington's response to the oil price shocks of the mid-70s with the three "strong reserve" countries of Germany, Switzerland, and Japan. All three of these countries import virtually 100% of their oil needs while the United States imports about 50%. So all three of these countries experienced even greater shocks from the oil prices than did the United States. But rather than permitting their monetary policies to accommodate the increase in the price of imported oil, these countries decided to bite the bullet then and endure some short-term economic problems for long-term economic growth and stability.

The United States, however, through its expansive monetary policies, accommodated the increase in the price of oil as the most politically acceptable method for allocating the burden through the economy. But as politically easy as this course of action seemed to be in the short-run, the last half of the 1970s showed the terrible price that Americans had to pay in the long-run. While inflation in the United States rose in double digit percentages, inflation in Germany, Switzerland, and Japan remained at less than one-half that rate. It was absolutely predictable that the decline in the value of the United States dollar against those three strong currency countries would be almost exactly equal to the difference in the comparative rates of inflation.

The American government's failure to bite the bullet with sound monetary policies during the 1970s, particularly as the country came out of the 1974 recession, enacted a terrible political and economic price for the public — a price which, in my judgment, could have been avoided by appropriate government action.

Perhaps most incongruous of all, as increasing levels of inflation have resulted in unprecedented rates of interest, low rates of growth and productivity, and a declining American competitive position, those who had been paying the steepest price were exactly those who were the targets of the misguided federal policies and lack of political discipline: the poor, young people seeking to buy a home for the first time, the elderly, and the American worker. I think it is clear today that the average American auto worker would rather have a job and low rates of inflation rather than billions of dollars in trade adjustment assistance while he sits unemployed as a result of our economic problems.

From these distasteful and difficult lessons of the 1970s, the American people are learning that there is a better way. The most heartening change, which will fundamentally affect the government policy, was the message of the American people on election day 1980 that it was time to change the direction of the United States economic policy. Eventually, the United States Congress sustained President Reagan's budget cuts almost to the dollar — such a fiscal policy by elected representatives of both parties would not have been possible before election day 1980.

While the president has been making progress on the spending cuts, government policy has been changing in other critical areas as well. The public is beginning to see progress in slowing down the deluge of complex federal regulations and even the repeal of some, as well as the partial or whole elimination of government subsidies that cover a variety of industries, agriculture, and services.

Delaware has seen the benefits of financial stability and tax reductions. While the full impact of these policies has yet been realized, we are sufficiently encouraged and heartened to maintain this political course and to improve upon it wherever possible. The same policies must be applied, on a far greater scale, to the federal government. Controlling inflation is the first imperative for revitalized American growth in the 1980s. But reduced tax burdens, reduced borrowing, regulatory reform, and energy independence will also be key elements in a national economic recovery.

Securing additional energy resources is a critical part of solving American economic problems. The United States must reduce its dependence on foreign oil for national security reasons, of course, but also because the cost of purchasing that oil requires tens of billions of dollars each year — money that the United States desperately needs for investment at home. The development of adequate domestic coal, nuclear, and oil resources thus becomes one of the two or three priorities of the nation. The time has come to begin that development with a new spirit, with the belief of the American people that it is time to change ineffective policies of the past, especially in energy resource production.

The challenge of the 1980s is to balance the protection of the environment, the encouragement of economic expansion, and the guarantee of energy independence. It can be done with intelligent consideration of the technical aspects of exploiting energy resources, especially the gas and oil beneath the sea, and appropriate government policies, America, stands on the threshold of a new opportunity — an opportunity to better the lives of all of its people. We must seize that opportunity before it is lost, so that the United States can continue to prosper and flourish.

Contents

THE FUTURE OF GAS AND OIL FROM THE SEA

Chapter 1
Petroleum from the Oceans: Resources, Exploration, and World Energy Role

Edgar S. Driver
B. P. Collins
H. Skolnick

The worldwide offshore oil potential is very large; and, therefore, of vital importance to the United States and other countries as their bridge to new energy sources that may be developed in the future. However, to make this potential for energy effective, exploration strategies for the recovery of offshore oil and gas must be applied on a regional (basin) scale. Moreover, to encourage exploration and development, leased blocks on the continental shelf and margins must be large enough to favor the probability of their containing both regional directional clues to the position of large fields, and, if the clues are positive, a portion of the potentially productive fairway.

No analysis of energy resources should begin without some sharp definitions, for considerable confusion exists over the use of geological terms by the media and politicians. In this chapter, *resource* means an undiscovered deposit of petroleum; *basin:* the fundamental geological unit within which petroleum is generated and concentrated; *regional:* dimensions corresponding to a major portion of a basin, typically hundreds of miles; *exploration strategy:* the net result of industry and government collaboration in finding and producing petroleum; and *fairway:* the concentration of large fields in a small part of a basin. There is also an assumption in this analysis that government's purpose in awarding offshore licenses is the prompt and efficient recovery of petroleum resources rather than immediate revenue alone.

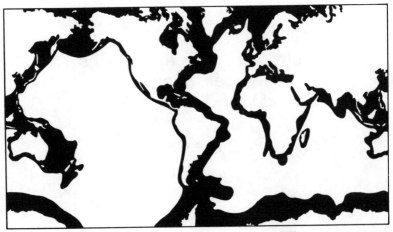

Continental Margins of the World

Map 1-1. Continental Margins.

OFFSHORE PETROLEUM RESOURCES

The prominent geomorphic features of the offshore areas of the world are shown in Map 1-1, *Continental Margins.* The areas of interest in petroleum prospecting consist of the *continental shelf,* the *continental slope,* the *continental rise,* the *small ocean basins.* Together they comprise about 80 million square kilometers, equivalent to about one-half the land area of the world. Prospects for petroleum accumulations in the central ocean regions are generally considered unfavorable because of thin sedimentary section.

Figure 1-1, *Worldwide Offshore Crude Oil Resources,* and Figure 1-2, *Worldwide Offshore Natural Gas Resources,* suggest the possible magnitude of offshore resources of crude oil and gas (with gas expressed as crude oil equivalents*). These figures project the resource magnitude in billions of barrels of annual production. One billion barrels of annual production equates to 2.74 million barrels of daily production. The total estimated resource can be determined by adding up the projected production rates for the years shown. The figures show two curves, one representing the worldwide total, combining

---

*5,604 cu. ft of gas = 1 barrel of oil

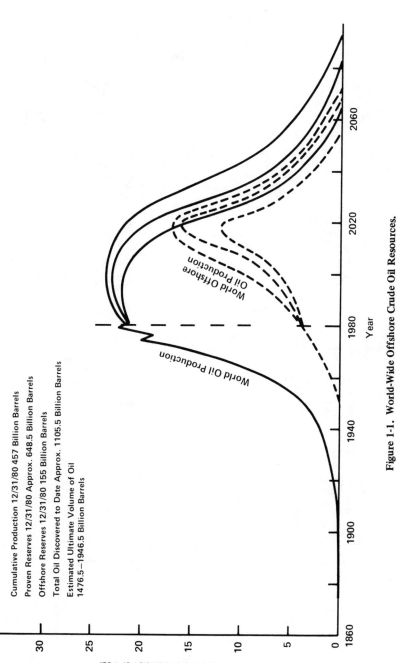

Cumulative Production 12/31/80 457 Billion Barrels

Proven Reserves 12/31/80 Approx. 648.5 Billion Barrels

Offshore Reserves 12/31/80 155 Billion Barrels

Total Oil Discovered to Date Approx. 1105.5 Billion Barrels

Estimated Ultimate Volume of Oil
1476.5–1946.5 Billion Barrels

World Oil Production

World Offshore
Oil Production

World Oil Production — Actual and Projected
in Billions of Barrels Per Year

Year

Figure 1-1. World-Wide Offshore Crude Oil Resources.

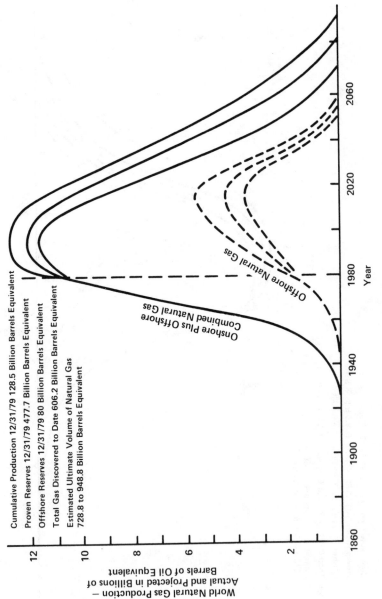

Figure 1-2. World-Wide Offshore Natural Gas Resources.

onshore and offshore resources and the other representing the offshore resources as a component of the total. Projected maximum offshore production ranges from 44 to 66 million barrels of oil and oil equivalents per day somewhere around the year 2020.

A sharp distinction must be drawn between what is known on these figures (to the left of the vertical line at 1980) and what is conjecture (to the right of that line). It is hazardous to use such estimates without a full understanding of their serious limitations. In the offshore case the uncertainty is great and for that reason the projections show a wide range of possible values rather than a single curve. For sound economic and political planning, drilling is needed to replace this conjecture with a factual inventory of deposits.

Figure 1-3, *Offshore Petroleum as Second Life Cycle in Petroleum Era,* also suggests that offshore oil and gas together may represent a second life cycle in the twentieth and twenty-first centuries. Some

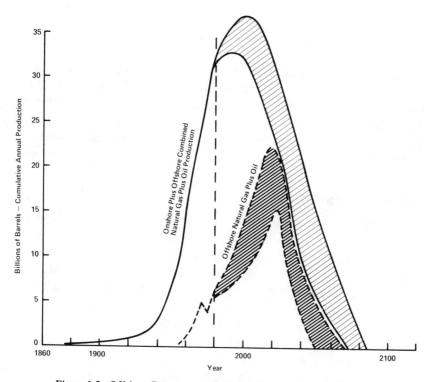

Figure 1-3. Offshore Petroleum as Second Life Cycle in Petroleum Era.

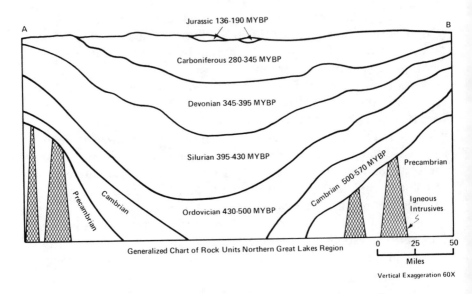

Figure 1-4. Sediments in Basin Form: Section.

experts believe there remains to be found as much oil and gas as has already been discovered and that the largest single source for the remainder lies in the offshore areas of the world. In any case, what has been learned since drilling for oil began in 1859 can be used to accelerate the recovery of the remaining resources in the continental margins of the earth.

EXPLORATION STRATEGIES

Exploration for new sources of offshore gas and oil must take into account, first of all, the geological factors that control gas and oil concentrations. In any area under consideration for drilling there must be a minimum thickness of sediments in basin form. Map 1-2, *Sediments in Basin Form,* and Figure 1-4, *Sediments in Basin Form: Section* illustrate the basin concept by means of the Michigan Basin, which shows the typical dimensions in a familiar context. These are horizontal and vertical views of the same basin. The position of the vertical view is shown by the line marked AB on the map. In the map of the Michigan Basin the outcropping sedimentary strata have been

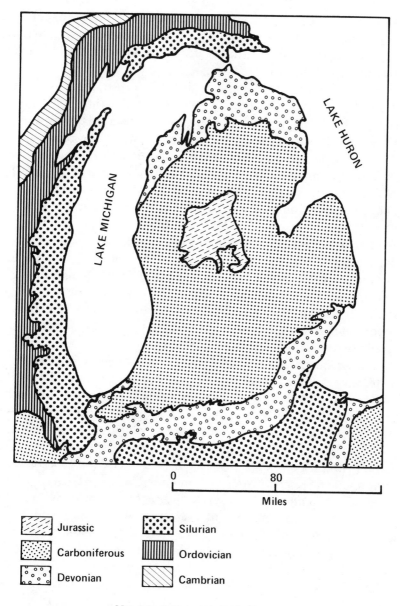

Map 1-2. Sediments in Basin Form.

shown and the center or deepest part of the basin has been indicated by the innermost Jurassic contour, representing the youngest rocks exposed. The outcropping strata become progressively older moving outward to the fringes of the basin.

The depth aspect of the basin is shown in Figure 1-4 by a vertical section. This is similar to the view of rock strata as they might be exposed in a road cut. In this case, however, the section portrays thousands of feet of superimposed sedimentary strata. The color coding of formations in Figure 1-4 is consistent with Map 2: The youngest rocks are top center and become older downward as well as outward. The floor of the basin is formed by rocks of igneous origin, which are not generally good prospects for petroleum. Offshore basins would have dimensions similar to the Michigan Basin.

A second major consideration in exploring for new sources of gas and oil is the character and structure of the sediments within a portion of a prospective basin. If there is to be an accumulation of oil, the sedimentary sequence must contain rocks that are rich in organic material of the proper kind. The basic organic material is known as kerogen, and one important type of this basic organic material is derived from planktonic algae. Moreover, the concentration of petroleum requires reservoirtype rocks. Sandstones and porous carbonates are examples where from a few percent to over 30% of the bulk volume of the rock consists of voids that can be filled with petroleum if it is available, although they are normally filled with water. These rocks are the reservoirs into which petroleum can migrate, where it can be stored, and from which it can be produced. The containment of petroleum also requires a specific geometric configuration of the reservoir rock and an impervious overlying cap rock. Figure 1-5, *Oil Traps,* shows several different types of traps: a structural anticlinal trap, entrapment against a salt dome, a fault trap, and a stratigraphic trap formed by pinchout of a reservoir rock.

To convey the petroleum as generated in the fine grained source rocks to the reservoir rocks and eventually to the traps, there must be faults, fractures or other permeable avenues. Fluids move through these conduits in response to fluid pressure differentials. It is common for these avenues of migration to open and close in response to the basic earth forces.

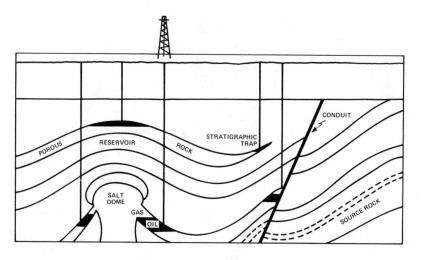

Figure 1-5. Oil Traps.

In sum, all of these ingredients must be present in the same general area and merge in a particular time sequence within the basin for reasonable expectations of discovering gas or oil or both, whether under dry land or in the continental margins under the sea.

EXPLORATION CONCEPTS

Over one hundred and twenty years of onshore exploration and production have revealed patterns of discovery that have been helpful in forming a strategy for offshore exploration. The following observations are very significant:

1. *Over 75% of the world's oil is contained within only 1% of the world's fields.* Map 1-3, *Onshore and Offshore Basins of the World* shows in black the locations of the basins containing these giant fields. The giant fields tend to be further localized within the basins in what are known as "fairways," where the largest concentrations occur, shown on the map in yellow.

2. *Generally the first significant discoveries in a new basin have been preceded by a long period of many dry holes.* This indicates the elusive character of oil concentrations and offers a challenge for

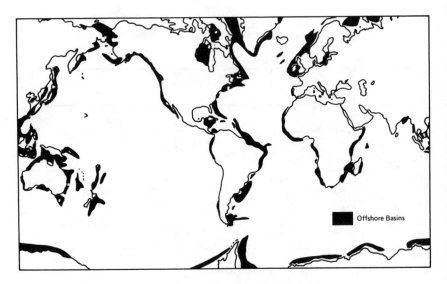

Map 1-3. Onshore and Offshore Basins of the World.

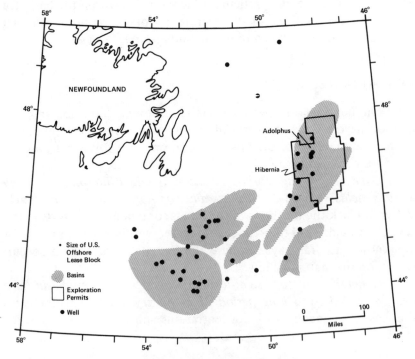

Map 1-4. The Avalon Basin.

improving the exploration technology. For example, several hundred dry holes were drilled in Western Canada before the Albertan fields were found. Map 1-4, *The Avalon Basin,* showing the east coast of Canada, provides a more recent offshore example. Dry holes are indicated by the ⊕ symbol and a concentration of oil wells by the yellow dot. The cluster of wells 200 miles east of Newfoundland at the yellow dot represents the recent Hibernia discovery. About 125 dry holes at 5 to 10 million dollars each were drilled before the fairway was found. The information from the dry holes eventually helped to guide the search to a really important find.

3. *After the first major discoveries in a productive basin, most of the big fields are found in a comparatively short period.* As an example about 60% of the oil in the Permian Basin of West Texas is in 70 major fields that were all found between 1930 and 1950.

NEW EXPLORATION TECHNOLOGY

The traditional exploration methods define only the most obvious requirements for accumulations; namely, thickness of sediments in basin form and major structures. These methods start with surface geology as a way to deduce subsurface structure from surface outcrops and this was followed by the geophysical methods of magnetic, gravity, and seismic surveying. Each geophysical method measures a different physical property of the subsurface rocks as a basis for a geological interpretation. The only known means for actually finding subsurface oil is still the drill itself.

In the past, the search for oil in large structures was only moderately successful as many structures were barren and subtle stratigraphic traps were overlooked. In recent years, however, there have been intensive efforts in the research laboratories and in field offices to understand more about the processes involved in concentrating petroleum and to develop geophysical methods for detecting the presence of hydrocarbons.

One of the most spectacular accomplishments of exploration seismology during the last ten years is known as the seismic bright spot technique. The seismic system can now detect the fact that when reservoir rocks are saturated with gas they have markedly different sonic and density properties than when they are in their normal water saturated state. Very strong seismic reflections are associated with gas reservoirs. This technique is effective for both structural and stratigraphic traps in the relatively unconsolidated rocks of Tertiary deltas. In these areas it has improved wildcat success ratios by a factor of three to four. Computers have played a vital role in the seismic bright spot technology and have been used in all the subsequent seismic developments.

The other major area of research seeks to understand the processes by which oil is concentrated, that is, how does generation, migration, and accumulation actually take place? How do we explain the powerful concentration mechanisms responsible for gathering 75% of the world's oil in only 1% of its fields.

The key concept in modern geochemistry that describes the thermal requirements for petroleum generation is shown in Figure 1-6, *Hydrocarbon Formation as a Function of Burial (Temperature)*. Flush oil generation from an organically rich source rock begins about 150°F and continues to over 300°F. Gas generation covers the same thermal window but continues to over 400°F. These temperatures correspond with different depths of burial within a basin depending on the basin's particular geothermal gradient.

This research helps us to use core, logs, and other data from dry holes as guides to productive fairways.

MARINE EXPLORATION TECHNOLOGY

Two major systems have been developed by the petroleum industry for offshore exploration, namely, marine geophysical vessels for reconnaissance exploration, and drilling rigs for a range of offshore water depths and sea conditions.

Geophysical research vessels are the pathfinders in offshore exploration. Their role is to gather the data needed to guide the drill to the most favorable sites. Illustrative of the state of the art is Gulf Oil's Research Vessel (R/V) *Hollis Hedberg,* which is 202 ft in length with a beam of 40 ft and 1,360 gross tons, shown in Figure 1-7. The vessel was constructed to ice class specifications. The diagram of the vessel shows the complement of geophysical, geological, and geochemical equipment aboard, which include the seismic, gravimeter, magnetometer, underwater seep detector, bottom corer, and computer systems.

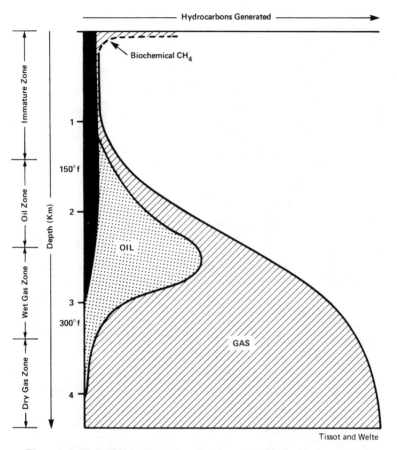

Figure 1-6. Hydrocarbon Formation as a Function of Burial (Temperature).

The onboard computer system is unique in that it performs a complete suite of sophisticated seismic programs such as would be carried out at an onshore seismic processing center. The purpose of this onboard processing system is to permit a complete geological evaluation in real time at sea. Figure 1-8, *Principle of Magnetic Method of Exploration;* Figure 1-9, *Principle of Gravity Method of Exploration;* Figure 1-10, *Principle of Seismic Method of Exploration,* and Figure 1-11, *Underwater Seep Detector,* illustrate exploration methods used on the R/V *Hollis Hedberg.*

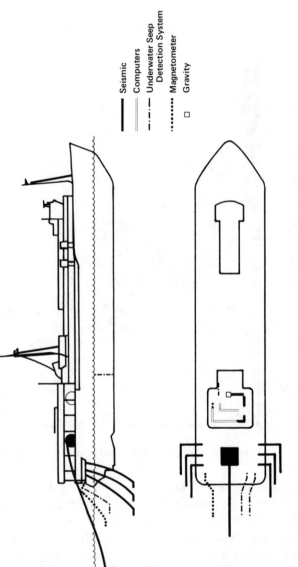

Seismic
Computers
Underwater Seep
    Detection System
Magnetometer
Gravity

Figure 1-7. The R/V HOLLIS HEDBERG Exploration Systems.

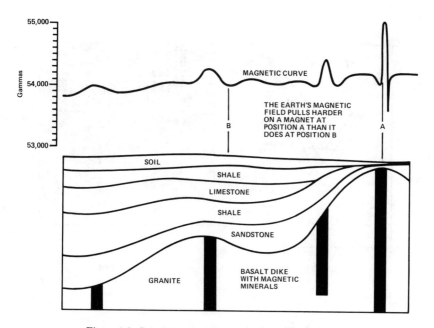

Figure 1-8. Principle of Magnetic Method of Exploration.

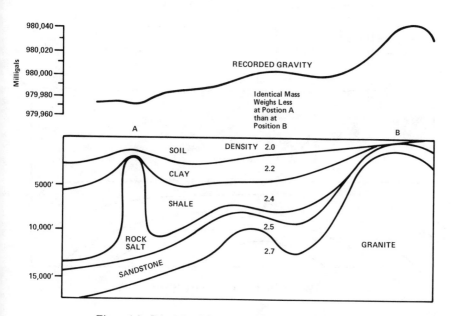

Figure 1-9. Principle of Gravity Method of Exploration.

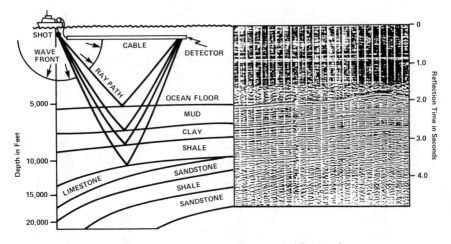

Figure 1-10. Principle of Seismic Method of Exploration.

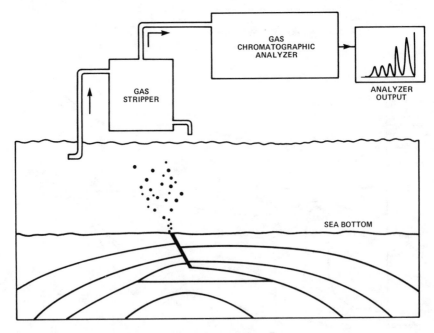

Figure 1-11. Underwater Seep Detector.

Interpretation of the data determines if the plan of data gathering should be altered to detail areas of special interest or to delete coverage of uninteresting regions. By combining reconnaissance and detailing in one cruise, the normal time delay between preliminary evaluation and follow-up drilling can be reduced by one season in frontier areas having limited seasonal access.

The R/V *Hollis Hedberg* and its predecessor, the R/V *Gulfrex* collected hundreds of thousands of miles of data over a 15-year period. These data combined with data gathered by oceanographic institutions and other oil companies form a vast network of control. The worldwide scope of this coverage and the geological interpretation of the data all derive from a plan developed by Dr. Hedberg in the mid-1960s. Because the vessel resulted from his prescience about the offshore areas as the last great petroleum frontier, it was named to honor him.

During this same period from the mid-1960s to the present, knowledge of marine and global geology was also advanced greatly by drilling. The Deep Sea Drilling Project (DSDP) was followed by the International Program of Ocean Drilling (IPOD). The R/V *Glomar Challenger*, carried out the DSDP-IPOD drilling.

To evaluate the offshore potential two factors must be examined: the results of drilling for petroleum, and the geophysical reconnaissance exploration of the undrilled remainder of the offshore. The most convincing evidence for the potential of gas and oil from offshore areas is the large amount of production from the relatively small portion of offshore areas drilled to date.

Twenty percent of worldwide petroleum production now comes from subsea basins and the major portion from the giant fields shown on Map 1-5, *Offshore Giant Fields*, by the large yellow dots.

The potential of the undrilled remainder of the offshore areas can be estimated by comparing what geophysical reconnaissance has shown with the known geological requirements for petroleum accumulation. First, the size and number of offshore basins revealed by geophysical reconnaissance compare favorably with onshore basins. Second, geophysical reconnaissance of the offshore basin has also shown that the incidence, magnitude, and nature of structures favorable for petroleum accumulation are comparable with the onshore

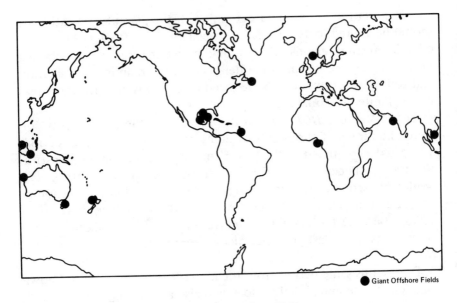

● Giant Offshore Fields

Map 1-5. Offshore Giant Fields.

basins. Third, the DSDP-IPOD holes drilled on the margins strongly suggest the presence of source and reservoir type rocks required for petroleum accumulations. In a recent AAPG paper, Hedberg, Moody, and Hedberg reported that 66% of the 133 DSDP-IPOD holes drilled on the continental margins and sampled for organic carbon contained some organic carbon in excess of the minimum required for an effective hydrocarbon source rock. Moreover, about 29% of these cores contained some reservoir quality sand. This is probably a low figure as sands tend to be lost in core recovery. Finally, there were 47 DEDP-IPOD holes that had shows of oil or gas, and that was from drilling that sought to avoid petroleum accumulations.

In sum, all the basic geological ingredients for the accumulation of gas and oil are in evidence in the offshore frontier basins of the world in ways unmistakenly similar to the onshore basins that have been drilled in the past century.

PLATE TECTONICS AND SEAFLOOR SPREADING

Map 1-5 shows how the offshore giant fields are located and found on the different kinds of continential margins. The margins are classified as *rifted* or, *convergent,* or may be *transform* according to their roles within the fundamental process by which continents and ocean floor are created.

Most of our current knowledge about marine geology derives from scientific exploration, conducted by oceanographic institutions, the government, and the petroleum industry during the last three decades. No truly global concept of geological processes would have been possible without the remarkable exploration of 70% of the earth's surface that is covered by water.

The great contribution of plate tectonics to petroleum geology has been the global view of tectonic and sedimentary processes. The geologic conditions that are favorable for the formation of good source bed and reservoirs of gas and oil are often global in character and contemporaneous in development. What is learned by drilling at great expense in one part of the world can be transferred to the early phases of exploration of a similar basin in another part of the world. Maps 1-6 and 1-7 show the South Atlantic and bordering South American and African continents. Map 1-6 represents the situation 140-150 MYBP in the Early Cretaceous age when only a narrow seaway separated the two continents. Map 1-7 shows the present situation.

During the late Juraassic to Early Cretaceous organically rich source rocks and reservoirs favorable for petroleum generation and containment were deposited in a lake environment. Large blocks of these rocks were attached to the two continents as they drifted apart after the initiation of the rising Mid-Atlantic ridge. Subsidence and thermal histories were roughly symmetrical astride the spreading center as the continents drifted apart. Today's map shows the location of the West African fields of Gabon, Angola, and Zaire, and the fields in a conjugate position offshore South America. There are many other areas throughout the world where similar geological reasoning can be effective.

OPTIMAL EXPLORATION STRATEGY

In simplest terms an optimal exploration strategy directs the search for petroleum to the productive fairways with a minimum of costly and time-consuming dry holes. While the sophisticated new technologies in geology, geophysics, and geochemistry extract important directional

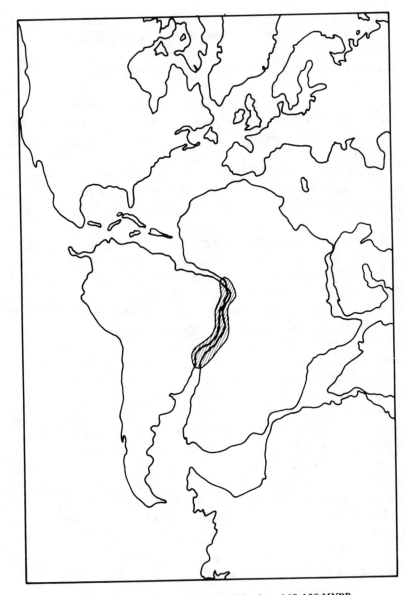

Map 1-6. Production on Conjugate Margins: 140-150 MYBP.

1. Recife Basin
2. Sergipe-Alagoas Basin
3. Jequitin Honha Basin
4. Espiritu Santos Basin
5. Campos Basin
6. Santos Basin
7. Congo Basin
8. Cuanza Basin

Map 1-7. Production on Conjugate Margins: Present.

clues from exploratory wells, there is ambiguity in single point de-
terminations. Like a problem in triangulation, it is still necessary to
have control from multiple directions and distances. By this rationale,
exploration must be regional in scope and highly technical in details
as positive steps towards an optimal exploration strategy.

Figure 1-12, *Stages of Exploration in Strategy — Persian Gulf,* illustrates the dimensions, stages, and direction of a regional exploration strategy. The famous fields of the Arabian Peninsula and the
Iranian fields are shown in section, and at the bottom of the section
the progressively smaller units of greater petroleum concentration
can be seen as the search is implemented from basin scale to fields.

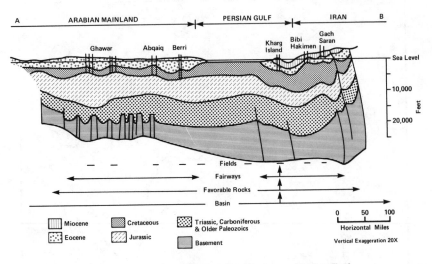

Figure 1-12. Stages of Exploration Strategy – Persian Gulf.

The development depicted in Figure 1-12 took over 50 years. On the basis of recent performances in the North Sea and West Africa, it seems clear that modern regional exploration strategies can substantially reduce the time needed for exploration and development. The current intensive exploration offshore China, and the development of the West Siberian oil province of the Soviet Union indicate that both Peking and Moscow understand the need for exploration strategy on a regional scale.

WORLD ENERGY ROLE AND SUMMARY

Gas and oil from offshore areas will play an important role in the future energy picture of the world. Figure 1-13, *U.S. Energy Usage,* illustrates the major impacts of the fuel alternatives, estimated in billions of barrels of oil equivalents, for the future energy needs of the United States alone. All energy sources will eventually be needed; in sequence and in proportion to their utility and economic viability. Much research will be needed before the synthetic fuels will be fully effective. In the intervening two to three decades, however, no energy alternative will combine size, economical feasibility, and quick recovery as well as offshore oil and gas. The effective recovery of

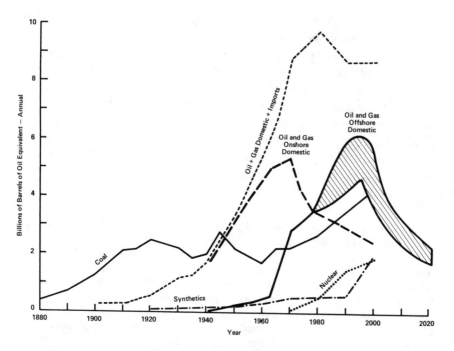

Figure 1-13. U.S. Energy Usage.

this resource can buy the time that is needed for systematic research and development of other energy resources.

In conclusion, *first,* the worldwide offshore petroleum potential is very large, a fact clearly indicated by offshore drilling and geophysical reconnaissance. Many experts believe that there is as much petroleum yet to be found as has been discovered to date and that the principal future source will be offshore areas. *Second,* to be effective, an exploration strategy for gas and oil must be conducted on a regional or basin scale. The basin is the fundamental geological unit within which hydrocarbons are generated and concentrated. *Third,* exploration and development blocks assigned to the search for petroleum must be large enough to favor the probability of their containing regional directional clues to major fields; then, if the clues are positive, they must contain a portion of the potentially productive fairway. In the area off Newfoundland, the exploratory well Adolphus, while uncommercial, proved the presence of petroleum and reservoir quality sands in the Avalon Basin and thus helped to point to the eventual major discovery of Hibernia in 1979. Both the indicator "dry hole" and the field were contained within a large assembly of development licenses available to a group of oil companies. By way of comparison the nine square mile size of U.S. offshore lease blocks is insufficient for implementation of a regional exploration strategy. The importance of regional exploration strategy has been very clear to foreign oil-producing countries where offshore leases average several thousands of square miles. Costly dry hole information and the ability to interpret it must be brought together with the incentive to risk the huge resources needed to develop the targeted fields.

Acknowledgments. The data and information compiled in this chapter represent the cumulative knowledge of the U.S. Continental Margin by many scientists from the U.S. Geogological Survey and academia. In particular John Schlee, John Grow, Bill Dillon, Kim Klitgord, Ray Martin, Jack Vedder, Dave McCulloch, Parke Snavely, George Plafker, Roland von Huene, Dave Scholl, Mike Fisher, Mike Marlow, Allan Cooper, and Art Grantz, of the U.S. Geological Survey, contributed greatly through unpublished data, publications, and direct assistance. Oswald Girard and Robert Towland reviewed the manuscript. The Resource Assessment Group, U.S. Geological Survey contributed to the resource assessment section and participated in discussions related to various basins. Margaret Goud, Mary Taylor, and Marti Nelson assisted in the preparation.

Chapter 2
Oil and Gas Resources of
the U.S. Continental Margin

N. Terrance Edgar

INTRODUCTION

In 1975 the U.S. Geological Survey (USGS) published estimates of the undiscovered recoverable oil and gas resources of both the on-shore and offshore (continental shelf only) areas of the United States, which represented a major effort that involved group appraisals by experts throughout the Geological Survey. The data and procedures used were documented and available for public inspection. Figure 2-1, *Petroleum Resource Classification,* clarifies the relationship of various terms that have been used in resource and reserve estimates. The USGS estimates and this analysis focus primarily on undiscovered re-coverable resources as indicated in the hachured box of Figure 2-1.

Estimates by the USGS were reported in terms of low, high, and mean values for the various provinces or groups of provinces assessed. All the estimates must be modified by a marginal probability to reflect the likelihood of the presence or absence of commercial accumulation.

In 1981, the USGS completed a new appraisal of conventionally producible crude oil and natural gas in the United States (Dolton et al., 1982) that incorporates new geologic information, new technological and economic considerations, and new or refined methods of resource appraisal.

The definitions in the new treatment remain the same, but the new estimates include separate values for the continental shelf less than 200 m (660 ft), and the continental slope, greater than 200 m and less than 2,400 m (7,920 ft) in Alaska and less than 2,500 m (8,250 ft) in the lower 48 states.

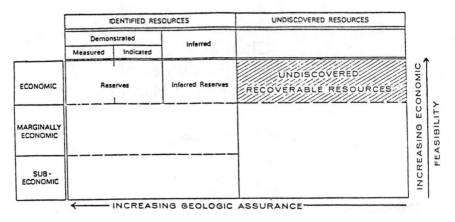

Figure 2-1. Petroleum Resource Classification.

Table 2-1, *Oil and Gas Estimates, U.S. Continental Shelf and Slope,* compares the total offshore estimates of oil and gas for 1975 and 1981.

There is little variation in the total estimates for oil, but the estimate for gas has doubled since 1975. The reason may be, in part, that the deep water area evaluated in 1981 was not considered in 1975. This represents an increase of 51% of the area previously assessed. In total, oil estimates for water depths less than 200 m (660 ft) were reduced by about 26^9 bbls, but these reductions were compensated for by the estimate of 28^9 bbls for the deep water environment. Table 2-2, *Conditional and Risked Mean Estimates of Undiscovered Recoverable Resources for the Outer Continental Shelf,* lists the basins in order of decreasing potential.

Table 2-1. Oil and Gas Estimates, U.S. Continental Shelf and Slope.

Oil in billions of barrels (bbl).
Gas in trillions of cubic feet (tcf).

	1975		1981	
	OIL 95%–5%	GAS 5%–5%	OIL 95%–5%	GAS 95%–5%
Continental Shelf	17–49	42–81	9–30	72–167
Continental Slope	–	–	4–19	29– 87
Total offshore	17–49	42–81	17–44	117–231

Table 2-2. Conditional and Risked Mean Estimates of Undiscovered Recoverable Resources for Outer Continental Shelf (OCS) Areas. (Listed in order of decreasing potential-statistical mean BOE*)

AREA	RANKING	MMBOE (RISKED)	OIL			GAS		
			CONDITIONAL MMBbls	MARGINAL PROBABILITY	RISKED MMBbls	CONDITIONAL Bcf	MARGINAL PROBABILITY	RISKED Bcf
Gulf of Mexico	1	18,473	6,500	1.00	6,500	71,840	1.00	71,840
Beaufort	2	14,688	7,930	1.00	7,930	40,430	1.00	40,430
Mid-Atlantic	3	5,410	3,490	0.87	3,040	14,220	1.00	14,220
So. California	4	3,020	2,360	1.00	2,360	3,960	1.00	3,960
Chukchi	5	2,540	2,840	0.51	1,450	8,600	0.76	6,540
North Atlantic	6	2,350	2,000	0.70	1,400	6,130	0.93	5,700
Navarin Basin	7	1,798	1,740	0.50	870	7,140	0.78	5,570
South Atlantic	8	1,612	1,650	0.60	990	4,440	0.84	3,730
Central and No. California	9	1,410	1,180	0.98	1,160	1,520	0.99	1,500
St. George Basin	10	803	1,480	0.28	410	4,280	0.55	2,360
Cook Inlet	11	790	400	1.00	400	2,340	1.00	2,340
Gulf of Alaska	12	710	1,000	0.36	360	3,180	0.66	2,100
Kodiak	13	658	1,000	0.33	330	3,230	0.61	1,970
Washington/Oregon	14	568	750	0.44	330	1,910	0.75	1,430
North Aleutian Shelf	15	377	990	0.21	210	2,370	0.42	1,000
Norton Basin	16	367	710	0.22	160	2,170	0.57	1,240
Shumagin Straits	17	180	400	0.20	80	1,400	0.43	600
Hope Basin	18	72	310	0.06	20	1,290	0.24	310

*Barrels of Oil Equivalent = BO + Mcfg/6 or MMBOE = MMBO + Bcfg/6

27

The new estimates compare favorably with the estimates prepared by others of undiscovered recoverable resources of liquid hydrocarbons and natural gas for both the onshore and offshore areas. Comparison of such are difficult because of a number of different assumptions, the definition of the areas, and the types of estimates used. Nevertheless, industry evaluations, although slightly lower, are comparable to those of the USGS. The estimates collectively reflect a consensus among major groups of professionals in the United States about the nation's future oil and gas resources.

The fundamental basis of any resource estimate is an understanding of the geology of the basin being assessed. In the offshore areas there is a wide range in the levels of understanding. In the following pages, each major offshore basin will be analyzed briefly in terms of its geology and the implications for the recovery of petroleum. The purpose will be to provide some tangible understanding of the basis for the resource estimates. In addition to an understanding of the geology of the basin, techniques such as extrapolation of historical trends, areal or volumetric yield methods, geochemical material, balance considerations, play analysis, and direct subjective team assessments have been employed to make assessments.

THE ATLANTIC MARGIN

The Atlantic margin is a classic example of a trailing passive margin characterized by pre-rift grabens, crustal thinning, and a later, clastic sequence. Initiation of continental breakup in the Triassic and Early Jurassic periods was marked by extension and the formation of grabens that roughly parallel the axis of rifting. A number of these grabens mapped onshore, such as the Connecticut Valley, can be traced offshore beneath the continental shelf. The late stage of rifting or the early stage of seafloor spreading is marked by Jurassic salt deposition on newly-formed oceanic crust.

The East Coast Magnetic Anomaly has identified the boundary between the continental and oceanic crusts. During the Jurassic, subsidence occurred in four areas along the U.S. Atlantic margin and these became the sites for the major deposition of clastic sediments on the landward part of the shelf, and carbonate sediments on the seaward part. A carbonate platform and paleoedge system of Jurassic and Early Cretaceous age extended the continental shelf breakup to 70 km seaward of its present location. Carbonate sedimentation in the middle and northern sectors came to a close in the Early Cretaceous period and was replaced by an influx of clastic sediments. Major shifts in sea level resulted in widespread unconformities in the Middle-Cretaceous, Tertiary, and Quaternary ages.

THE ATLANTIC REEF

From the interpretation of early seismic refraction studies off the Atlantic margin, Maurice Ewing and his colleagues identified thick sedimentary basins beneath the continental shelf and a thick sedimentary prism beneath the continental rise. The two are separated by a structure of high seismic velocity, which was interpreted as a basement high. On the basis of seismic reflection data, Emery reinterpreted the refraction studies and concluded that the "basement" high might be carbonate instead. Subsequently many investigators have presented seismic evidence in support of the carbonate interpretation and have interpreted some structures as reefs.

Recently, samples of reefal carbonates have been recovered from outcrops in canyons cutting the continental slope off Georges Bank. The COST B-3 well penetrated carbonates that may represent a back reef facies in the Baltimore Canyon Trough, and the *Glomar Challenger* recovered reefal carbonates from the eastern edge of the Blake Plateau. On the basis of seismic stratigraphic relationships and these samples, the carbonates are believed to be predominantly Jurassic but to extend into the Early Cretaceous period.

Figure 2-2, *Jurassic/Cretaceous Reef Trend,* shows the location of the carbonate trend; the solid line indicates where the reef is believed to be well developed. Figure 2-3, *Location of Reef Trend through the Baltimore Canyon,* shows in detail the relationship of the reef trend along the continental slope, the COST wells and the lease blocks, and Figure 2-4, *Baltimore Canyon Trough,* demonstrates the relationship between the reef and the surrounding sedimentary basins. Note that the reef has prograded seaward and is interpreted as overlying oceanic crust.

These reefs appear to be part of a major trend extending as a discontinuous feature from the Canadian Atlantic continental margin,

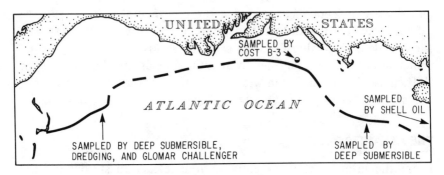

Figure 2-2. Jurassic/Cretaceous Reef Trend.

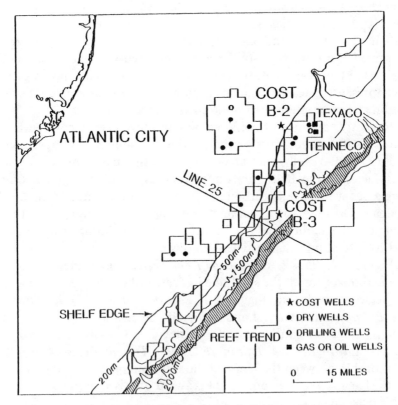

Figure 2-3. Location of Reef Trend through the Baltimore Canyon Trough.

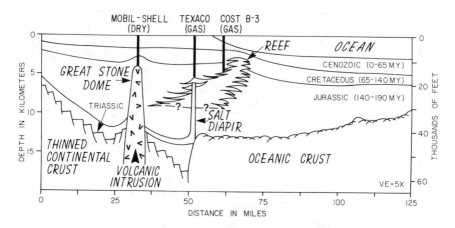

Figure 2-4. Baltimore Canyon Trough.

south along the U.S. margin to the Bahamas, northwest across the West Florida Platforms, through Texas and south to the petroleum rich reefs of the Golden Lane and Gulf of Campeche in Mexico, as shown in Figure 2-5, *Jurassic-Cretaceous Reef Trend, Canada to Mexico.* In Canada the reefs rarely exhibit porosity; and where they do, they do not contain petroleum. In contrast, the Mexican reefs were raised above sea level where the porosity was greatly enhanced through fresh water solution. The reefs then were buried and formed outstanding reservoirs.

Of critical importance in evaluating the petroleum potential of the U.S. Atlantic reefs is whether they underwent a history similar to that of the Mexican reefs or that of Canada. These are the end members and a full spectrum of possibilities lies in between.

In addition to the possibilities the reef presents, the discovery in the deep Atlantic basins of widespread organic rich clays of early Cretaceous age presents a possible source rock of great importance. Seismic evidence is consistent with the idea that these strata extend beneath the continental rise and slope and terminate against, or close to, the reef. However, it has been pointed out, much of the organic material is of terrestrial origin, oxidized and thermally immature. Where it was sampled, it was believed to be unsuitable as a source rock for oil, but, buried beneath the continental margin, it could generate

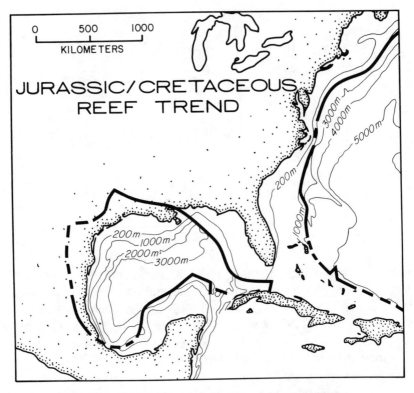

Figure 2-5. Jurassic/Cretaceous Reef Trend, Canada to Mexico.

gas. Whether the thick wedge of Jurassic sediment underlying these clays contains suitable source rocks is unknown.

GEORGES BANK

Oil (10^9 bbls)	Gas (tcf)
Mean	Mean
1.4	5.7

The Georges Bank is an irregular basin or a collection of subbasins, of which some are linear grabens. The bank lies between the La Have Platform, the Gulf of Maine Platform, and the Long Island Platform.

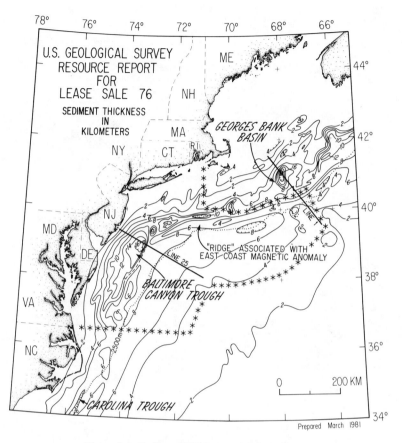

Figure 2-6. Sediment Thickness of Georges Bank.

The deepest part of the basin contains the oldest sediments; it is located in a restricted rectangular depression in the south central part
shown in Figure 2-6, *Sediment Thickness of Georges Bank.*

A schematic cross-section of the Georges Bank is shown in Figure
2-7, *Georges Bank Area.* The figure was prepared utilizing seismic,
magnetic, gravity, and COST well data. The COST G-1 well penetrated a thick clastic sequence of Late Jurassic to Early Tertiary age
that overlies sandstone, anhydrite, and dolomite of Early or Middle
Jurassic age. The COST G-2 well, shown in Figure 2-8, *Lithographic
Logs of Cost Wells,* was drilled 67 km (40 miles) to the east of G-1

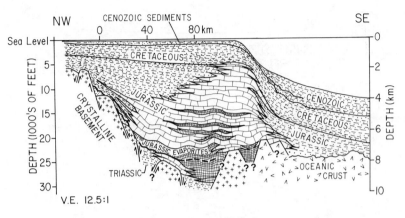
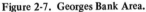

Figure 2-7. Georges Bank Area.

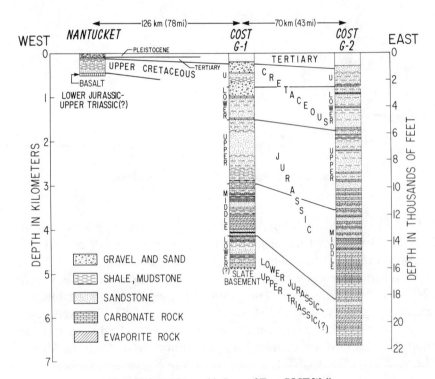

Figure 2-8. Lithographic Logs of Two COST Wells.

well and penetrated a thick section containing more carbonate and evaporite rocks than were found in G-1. The Upper Jurassic to Tertiary section is composed primarily of mudstones and sandstones although the Lower Cretaceous sequence contains thick beds of limestone that are presumably a part of a carbonate bank/reef complex that develops more fully seaward.

The organic content in the COST G-1 well, between 1400 and 1900 m (4,620 and 6,270 ft), is sufficiently high for the rock to be considered a potential source rock. Although the section contains oil and gas-prone kerogen types, these are thermally immature. The entire sedimentary section of the COST G-2 well may contain enough organic carbon to be considered a potential source; rock providing 0.2 percent by weight of organic carbon is considered adequate. If not, then the source rock potential of the section below 3,000 m (9,600 ft) is probably marginal.

Structures suitable for trapping petroleum in Georges Bank are primarily compactional structures over buried basement blocks, carbonate buildups and salt swells.

MID-ATLANTIC AREA

Oil (10^9 bbls)	Gas (tcf)
Mean	Mean
3.1	14.2

The isopach map in Figure 2-6 shows the configuration of the Baltimore Canyon Trough. Line 25 in Figure 2-9, *The Baltimore Canyon,* shows the location of a cross-section across the trough. The cross-section suggests that the trough is built over a zone of rifted, thinned continental crust (transitional crust). Pre-rift Triassic red beds and volcanics are shown overlain by thin evaporites. The bulk of the sedimentation occurred in the Jurassic age beneath the continental shelf, slope, and upper rise. Clastic sediments filled the western part of the basin in the Jurassic age while the carbonate bank to the east became well developed and appears to be capped by an extensive prograding reef complex. Earlier interpretations suggested that the reef grew on a basement high, but some recent analyses suggest that in

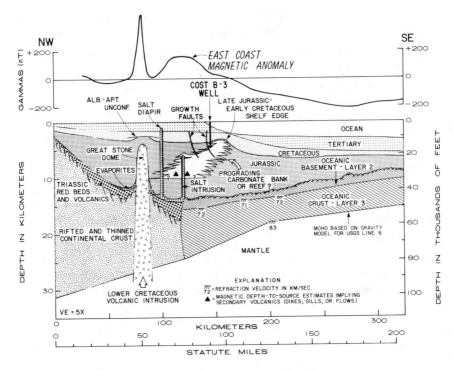

Figure 2-9. Baltimore Canyon Trough.

some areas there may be no basement high underlying the carbonate bank.

In the Early Cretaceous age, a mafic intrusion (the Great Stone Dome) invaded the basin, setting the stage for possible hydrocarbon accumulation. In addition, a salt diapir was discovered in the trough by a seismic survey.

The reef and carbonate bank gave way in the Early Cretaceous age to clastic sedimentation that dominated the sedimentary sequence until the present.

The COST B-2 well (Figure 2-10, *Exploratory Wells in the Baltimore Canyon Trough,* and Figure 2-11, *Geological Cross-Section of Baltimore Canyon Trough*) drilled on the shelf penetrated 4,800 m (16,000 ft) of sediments and terminated in the Upper Jurassic stratum. The Jurassic and Early Cretaceous sediments are predominantly non-marine clastics, but these graded to a shallow marine environment in

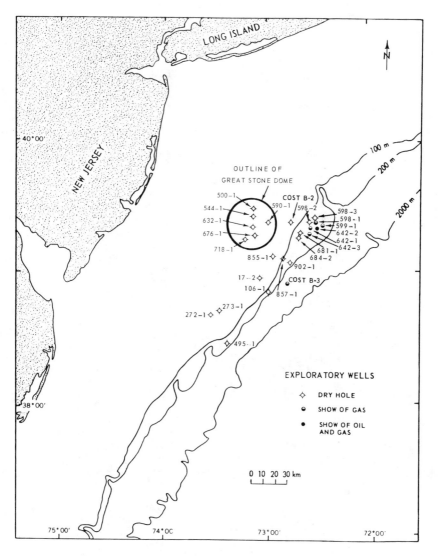

Figure 2-10. Exploratory Wells in Baltimore Canyon Trough.

the Late Cretaceous age (with the exception of a nonmarine interval during the Coniacian and Santonian). The Tertiary clastic rocks are characteristic of both inner and outer shelf environments.

The sediments recovered in the COST B-2 well are rich in predominantly terrestrial organic matter, but to a depth of 3,680 m (12,000 ft) they are immature. The porosities and permeabilities of

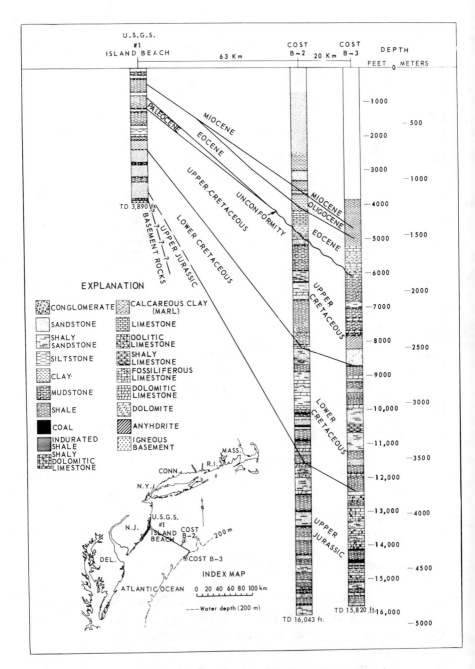

Figure 2-11. Geological Cross-Section of Baltimore Canyon Trough.

the clastics decrease with increasing depth primarily because of authigenic clay and silica cement.

The COST B-3 well was drilled on the Continental Slope in 819 m (2,686 ft) of water to a depth of 4,822 m (15,820 ft) below the platform. The organic carbon is thermally immature to a depth of 4,359 m (14,300 ft). Below this depth, gas-prone organic carbon is thermally mature and a small show of gas was encountered.

By the summer of 1981, there were 25 exploratory wells drilled in the Baltimore Canyon Trough, as shown in Figure 2-10, and significant hydrocarbon shows had been reported from the following five wells.

Texaco	598-1	gas
Texaco	642-1	gas
Texaco	642-3	gas
Tennaco	642-2	oil/gas
Exxon	599-1	gas

The largest and most promising structure, the Great Stone Dome, was drilled by six wells, but no discoveries had been reported.

The drilling data suggest that the hydrocarbon potential of the shelf area is low, but it may be better near the shelf edge. The increase in the number of shows near the carbonate/reef complex suggests that the best prospects may be associated with these carbonates lying beneath the slope.

SOUTH ATLANTIC AREA

Oil (10^9 bbls)	Gas (tcf)
Mean	Mean
0.9	3.6

There are three sedimentary basins in the South Atlantic area: The Southeast Georgia Embayment, the Carolina Trough, and the Blake Plateau basin are shown in Figure 2-12, *Basins of U.S. Southeastern Continental Margin.* The latter two were major centers of deposition, accumulating 13 km (42,900 ft) in the Blake Plateau and 12 km (39,600 ft) in the Carolina Trough (Figure 2-13, *Thickness of Sedimentary*

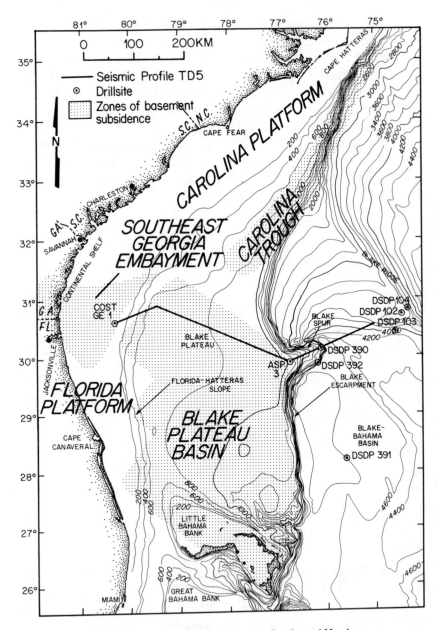

Figure 2-12. Basins of U.S. Southeastern Continental Margins.

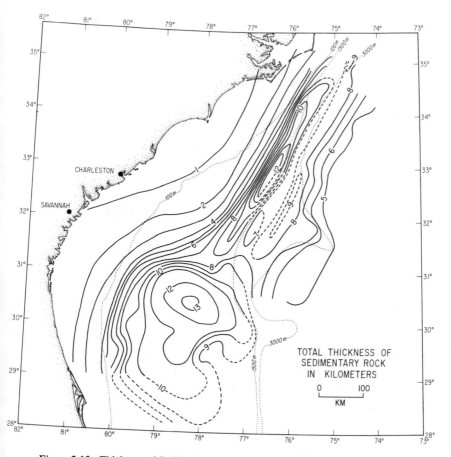

Figure 2-13. Thickness of Sedimentary Rock-Offshore Southeastern United States.

Rock — Offshore Southeastern United States). The Southeast Georgia Embayment is a relatively minor crustal sag that extends onshore beneath the Atlantic Coastal Plain.

Development of this continental margin began with the onset of rifting in the Triassic and Early Jurassic time (Figure 2-14, *Sections of Florida Platform, Blake Plateau, and Blake Basin*). An extensive area, later to become Blake Plateau Basin, was subjected to tension, rifting, stretching, and intrusion, but, before ocean crust actually formed, the spreading center shifted eastward of the plateau where the new ocean crust emerged. The thinned crust subsided rapidly,

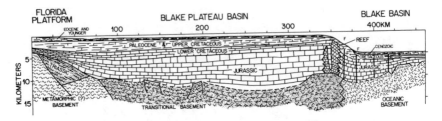

Figure 2-14. Sections of Florida Platform, Blake Plateau, and Blake Basin.

and reefs grew over extensive areas during the Jurassic age. In the Early Cretaceous period, reef growth was terminated, but the area continued to subside, increasing the water depth. Carbonate sedimentation continued westward as chalks and marls into the Southeast Georgia Embayment. By the end of the Paleocene age, the Gulf Stream actively eroded the inner plateau and prevented sedimentation on the outer plateau.

The COST GE-1 well (Figure 2-15, *COST GE-1 Well*) encountered Paleozoic rocks at 3,300 m (10,560 ft) that are overlain by probable Jurassic nonmarine clastics and coal and dolomite and anhydrite. This sedimentary regime continued into the late Early Cretaceous age when marine carbonate sedimentation was initiated, and extended to the Holocene period.

Six dry holes were drilled in the embayment. Source rocks in the arc are poor, according to the results of the COST GE-1 well. Rocks at depths are predominantly continental, and the overlying marine sequence lies at depths less than 1,000 m (3,200 ft). There are very few attractive structures, other than a few drape structures overlying basement irregularities.

The inner part of the Blake plateau basin has a much thicker sedimentary section that is probably dominated by marine rocks, indicating a better environment for finding source rocks. Stratigraphic traps and pinchouts against basement rocks are trap possibilities, but the regional landward dip across the basin would suggest a general sediment migration to the east where reefs and carbonate banks structures could serve as reservoirs and traps.

The Carolina Trough is a long, narrow depression of thinned continental crust that developed during the initiation of continental

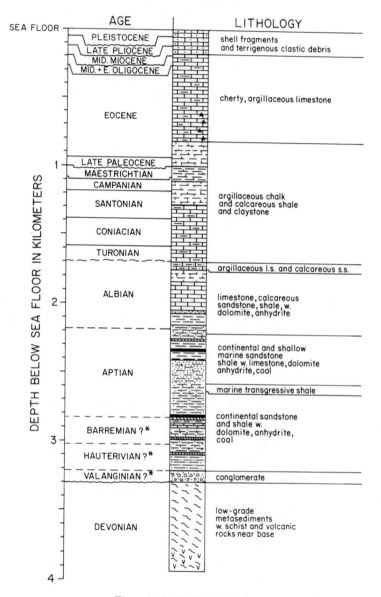

Figure 2-15. COST GE-1 Well.

rifting. During the Jurassic age, a thick layer of salt was deposited and then covered by a thick accumulation of sediment that gave rise to salt diapirism. Cenozoic sedimentation was limited by the erosive action of the Gulf Stream.

Because no wells have been drilled in the Carolina Trough, little can be said regarding the presence of source rocks other than the inference that sedimentation was most likely marine. The salt domes and associated fault structures provide the most likely traps, but these are located under more than 3,000 m (9,600 ft) of water.

GULF OF MEXICO

	Oil (19^9 bbls)	Gas (tcf)
	Mean	Mean
Eastern Gulf of Mexico	0.2	0.5
Western Gulf of Mexico	2.4	26.1

The oil and gas resources of the Gulf of Mexico in this analysis have been restricted to the deep-water areas of the continental slope (deeper than 200 m or 660 ft) that represent the frontier areas. Figure 2-16 shows two areas, an eastern and a western slope, for which separate resource estimates have been made. Suffice it to say for the remainder of the Gulf that 4.76 billion barrels of oil and 39 trillion cubic feet of gas have been produced, and the most recent estimates of undiscovered oil and gas for the continental shelf alone are about 4.0 billion barrels of oil and 45 trillion cubic feet of gas.

Figure 2-17 is a cross-section through the west central part of the Gulf of Mexico showing a trough of major deposition beneath the Gulf Coastal Plain and the Continental Shelf. However, almost the entire slope from the Mississippi Fan to northeastern Mexico is underlain by a massive wedge of salt capped by a variable but predominantly relatively thin cover of sediment (Figure 2-18). The salt has intruded the sediment in many styles and created hummocky topography and many shallow to thick sedimentary basins. Shallow core holes drilled by the Shell Oil Development Company demonstrated that Jurassic and Upper Cretaceous sediments overlie salt plugs on the slope. The southern rim of the salt is marked by the Sigsbee Escarpment, and

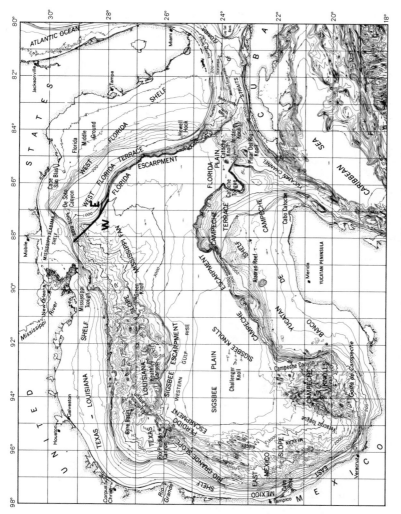

Figure 2-16. Bathymetry of Gulf of Mexico Region.

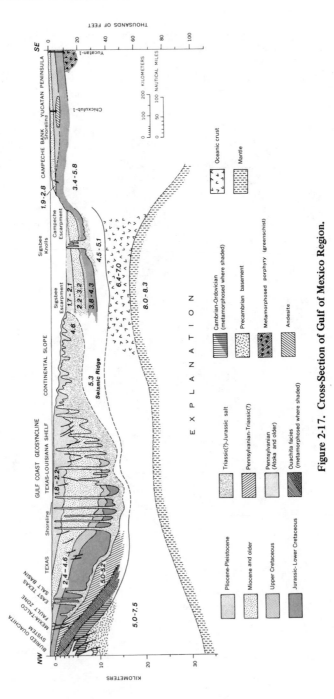

Figure 2-17. Cross-Section of Gulf of Mexico Region.

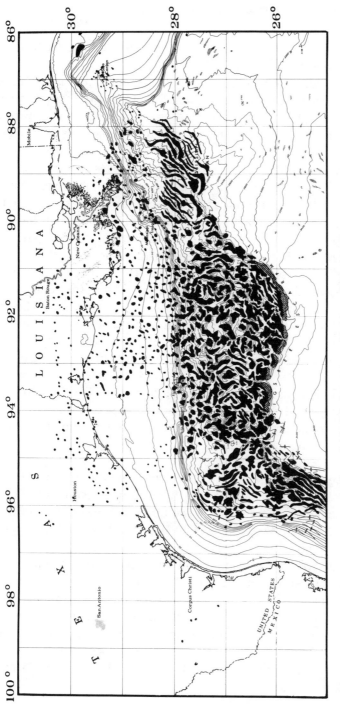

Figure 2-18. Salt Structures – Northern Gulf of Mexico.

there is evidence that the salt has overridden sedimentary beds of the Sigsbee Abyssal Plain (Figure 2-18).

In the middle slope region of the Mississippi Fan there is a system of northeast-trending salt anticlines 1 to 15 km (0.6 to 10 miles) in breadth and 30 to 140 km (20 to 90 miles) in length. Narrow troughs containing as much as 2,000 m or more of sediment lie between those ridges.

To the east, salt structures beneath the Texas-Louisiana Slope are of two types: broad stocks and ridges distributed in a random pattern in the middle slope region, and relatively low relief structures rising only a few hundred meters above the main salt body. In the middle slope region, the salt stocks and ridges are separated by deep sediment-filled troughs, whereas the sediment cover in the lower slope region is relatively thin, less than 2,000 m (6,500 ft).

On the continental slope off South Texas, the structural character of the salt intrusions is very different from that of the Texas-Louisiana Slope. Most of the area is underlain by a shallow salt layer with a mildly deformed upper surface. The exception is the upper slope region around Alaminos Canyon where salt anticlines and stocks are common features.

The oil and gas potential of the slope west of the De Solo Canyon is relatively good, as indicated by the thickness of sediment, an abundance of structures, and proximity to major sedimentary sources. However, there are large areas where massive salt is overlain by relatively thin sediment that is probably not very attractive.

The deep abyssal plain also has oil and gas potential, but it has not been taken into consideration in these resource estimates. The sediment thickness reaches 9,150 m (30,000 ft) at the edge of the Sigsbee Escarpment. The Mesozoic section is probably buried too deeply to have much potential for oil and gas, but the pre-Pliocene Tertiary sediments, consisting of muds and sandy turbidites, may have potential. The sandstones may be suitable as reservoirs, and, if so, would greatly enhance the resource potential of the area. Source rocks are apparently present and thermally mature, as indicated by the recovery of oil from a core of cap rock taken by the *Glomar Challenger* from Challenger Knoll. Broad but low relief, anticlines, and small displacement faults are common throughout the region and could provide traps for petroleum.

In particular the Perdido Foldbelt located in the abyssal plain at the foot of the South Texas slope appears most prospective. The fold-belt consists of large, mostly buried anticlines of well-layered strata folded over a core of salt. The folds are about 2.5 to 5.6 km (1.5 to 3.5 miles) in width and about 49 km (30 miles) long. Up to 3,650 m (12,000 ft) of Cretaceous and Tertiary rocks are folded and overlain by 1,220 m (4,000 ft) of younger sediments. The distance between the structures ranges from 4,880 m to about 6,400 m (16,000 to 21,000 ft).

SOUTHERN CALIFORNIA

	Oil (10^9 bbls)	Gas (tcf)
	Mean	Mean
Santa Barbara	1.3	2.5
Inner Basins	0.6	0.5
Outer Basins	0.5	0.9

The ridge and basin structure characteristic of the Southern California Borderland shown in Figure 2-19, *Southern California Border-land and Basement Terranes,* is attributed to the right lateral shear which began along the boundary between the Pacific and North American Plates about 30 million years ago. Subsequent erosion of the ridges resulted in thick sedimentation in the basins. These sediments were locally folded and faulted by right shear that has continued to the present.

In the Santa Barbara Channel, the Cretaceous and Lower Tertiary strata are thick, deep-sea, fan deposits that grade into younger Paleogene rocks of shallow to nonmarine origin. Lower Miocene shales and silts were deposited under deepening marine conditions, and by upper Miocene organic-rich muds that were being deposited. Thick sequences of Pliocene turbidites were deposited in the northern and northeastern part of the basins, but these deposits may thin to the south and southwest.

The primary source rock is believed to be the fine-grained sediments of Miocene and Pliocene sandstones and fractured Miocene Monterey Formation.

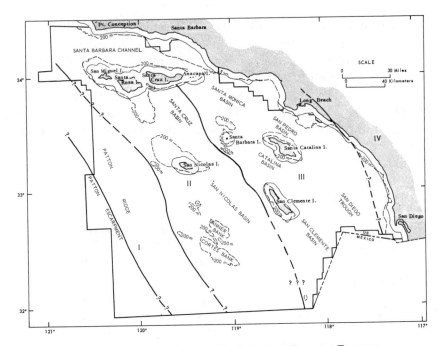

Figure 2-19. Southern California Borderland and Basement Terranes.

The inner basins and bank of the Borderland (terrane III) extend from the Santa Barbara Channel on the north to the U.S.-Mexican boundary to the south and include three major basins: the Santa Monica and San Pedro basins, and the Gulf of Catalina/San Diego trough. The Miocene Monterey shale is the oldest sedimentary unit overlying a volcanic and schist basement (Catalina Schist) in the Santa Monica basin, where the Neogene sections may reach 2400 m (8,000 ft). In the San Pedro basin, Miocene sedimentary rocks also overlie schists and volcanic rocks but only in the northern part does the section attain 900 m (3,000 ft). This section thins to the southwest and may be absent in the central part of the basin where a thick Pliocene section overlies the basement.

To the south, the eastern margins of the Gulf of Catalina and San Diego Trough may be underlain by thick Upper Cretaceous Paleogene rocks. To the west the Miocene sediments directly overlie the Catalina Schists and volcanic rocks.

The outer basins and banks are underlain by two pre-Neogene basement slices: an inner belt or terrane II (Santa Rose-Cortes Ridge and Santa Cruz and San Nicolas Basins) that forms of the "Great Valley" sequence, and the outer belt or terrane I (continental slope and Patton Ridge) that correlates with the Franciscan Complex. Upper Cretaceous rocks have been sampled in a wide area overlying the "Great Valley" sequence. For example, the deep stratigraphic test well (OCS-CAL 75-70 No. 1) drilled near the southeast end of Cortes Bank penetrated nearly 1200 m (4,000 ft) of Upper Cretaceous sandstone.

In addition, the well penetrated about 580 m (1905 ft) of Middle and Lower Miocene rocks, 170 m (567 ft) of basaltic flows (Oligocene age), 400 m (1340 ft) of Oligocene sediments, 560 m (1950 ft) of Eocene rocks, and 270 m (850 ft) of Paleocene rocks.

Eocene rocks underlie most of the Santa Rose-Cortes Ridge and extend south to Tanner and Cortes Banks. Although they underlie the western edge of both the Santa Cruz and San Nicolas Basins to the east, it is doubtful they are found in the eastern part of these basins. No Paleogene rocks have been sampled south of Cortes Bank.

Miocene sediments are distributed widely on the outer Borderland shelves and slopes and in the large outer basins may allow a thickness of 1500 m (5000 ft) of possible turbidites.

The structure of the Borderland is characterized by many broad anticlines that lie oblique to major fault zones. Although there are few structures in the centers of the large basins, major upwarps near the edges of the basins cause numerous minor folds.

Two of the largest onshore petroleum basins west of the San Andreas fault extend offshore into the southern California offshore area. The Ventura Basin extends beneath the prolific Santa Barbara Channel, and the Los Angeles Basin beneath the inner Borderland. The cumulative production from all onshore California coastal basins to 1975 totalled 9.9 billion barrels of oil; the remaining reserves, including indicated reserves from proven fields, were estimated to be 2.3 billion barrels (American Petroleum Institute, 1975).

Despite the production from onshore fields adjacent to the Borderland, only the Beta field in the San Pedro Basins has been developed. In the outer part of the Borderland, the data from the stratigraphic test well, OCS-CAL 75-70 No. 1, drilled at Cortes Bank appeared most promising, but subsequent exploratory drilling was disappointing.

Potential source rocks occur in upper Eocene and Miocene rocks, but the organic matter is immature. These organic-rich rocks may have matured in the central parts of the basins where they are deeply buried, and the petroleum generated could have migrated to the small folds found along the margins of the basins. The source rock and reservoir rock potential of the lower Eocene, Paleocene, and Cretaceous ages are not promising.

Seismic data indicate that 1500 m (5000 ft) of Miocene rocks may be present in the large outer basins. The *Glomar Challenger* drilled site 467 in San Miguel Gap and recovered Miocene rocks with good source rock potential. In addition, sandy turbidites in the middle Miocene through the Pliocene section may be potential reservoirs.

NORTH AND CENTRAL CALIFORNIA

	Oil (10^9 bbls)	Gas (tcf)
	Mean	Mean
Santa Maria Basin	0.7	1.7
Outer Santa Cruz Basin	0.2	0.2
Bodega Basin	Negl.	Negl.
Point Arena	0.1	Negl.
Eel River Basin	Negl.	Negl.

In the Late Cretaceous time, the then northern and central California margin was under the tectonic influence of the subducting Farallon plate, which lay between the North American and Pacific plates. The Farallon plate was totally destroyed in the process, and the North American and Pacific plates came in contact, altering the tectonic setting from one of subduction to one of strike-slip.

Currently, strike-slip motion dominates western California south of Cape Mendocino, but to the north of the Cape, the Pacific crust is being subducted. The formation of five shelf basins of northern and central California may be attributed to wrench tectonics. These basins are, from south to north, the Santa Maria, Outer Santa Cruz, Bodega, Point Arena and Eel River basins, which are shown in Figure 2-20, *Basins and Exploratory Wells – Northern California.*

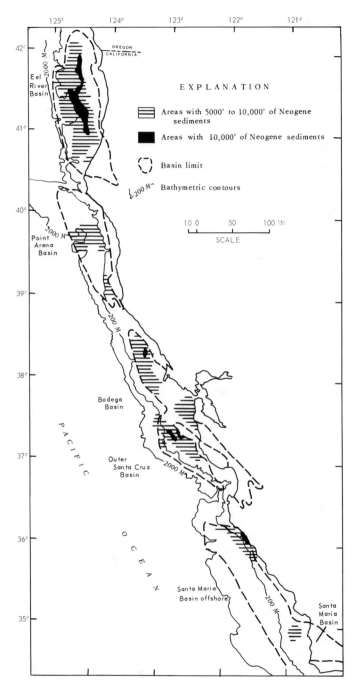

Figure 2-20. Basins and Exploratory Wells – Northern California.

Table 2-3. Exploratory Wells Drilled on OCS Lands (after 1963 Federal OCS Lease Sale).

COMPANY	AND WELL NAME	BASIN	TOTAL DEPTH		SPUDDED	ABANDONED
			METERS	FEET		
Humble	P-012-1	Eel River	9034	2964	7-30-64	8-19-64
Humble	P-007-1	Eel River	273	897	7-01-64	7-27-64
Shell	P-019-1ET	Eel River	1981	6500	7-11-65	7-30-65
Shell	P-014-1ET	Eel River	2249	7377	6-17-65	7-7-65
Shell	P-032-1ET	Point Arena	2106	6909	11-26-66	1-13-67
Shell	P-033-1ET	Point Arena	1438	4719	10-24-66	11-11-66
Shell	P-030-1ET	Point Arena	3242	10,636	3-10-65	6-10-65
Shell	P-027-1ET	Bodega	986	3234	11-17-64	11-29-64
Shell	P-058-1ET	Bodega	2402	7882	1-18-67	2-07-67
Shell	P-053-1ET	Bodega	2456	8059	12-2-64	12-26-64
Shell	P-055-1ET	Bodega	2279	7477	10-12-64	11-6-64
Shell	P-055-2ET	Bodega	2213	7261	1-3-65	1-23-65
Shell	P-055-2AET	Bodega	2224	7297	1-25-65	2-15-65
Shell	P-051-2ET	Bodega	3190	10,466	8-2-64	10-3-64
Shell	P-041-1ET	Bodega	1433	4700	9-20-63	12-13-63
Shell	P-039-1ET	Bodega	1717	5632	2-16-65	3-3-65
Shell	P-036-1ET	Outer Santa Cruz	2283	7490	2-10-67	3-17-67
Shell	P-035-1ET	Outer Santa Cruz	2357	7736	9-01-67	9-28-67
Humble	P-060-1	Santa Maria	2444	8020	9-29-64	1-08-65

Nineteen exploratory wells and one COST well (OCS-CAL 78-164 No 1) have been drilled in these basins. Table 2-3 is a listing of the wells drilled in each basin. None produced oil or gas.

The Santa Maria Basin is an offshore segment of the onshore, petroleum-producing Santa Maria basin. The basement of the offshore basin is probably Franciscan, but there are some investigators who believe it may be granite. The basement is overlain by what are perceived to be erosional remnants of Paleogene rocks. A Middle Tertiary unconformity marks the beginning of substantial Miocene and Pliocene sedimentation. The Miocene section is dominated by siliceous shales and cherts, the equivalent of the Monterey Formation on land. These are overlain by Pliocene marine siltstone and claystone.

Folds and faults in the northern part of the basin trend parallel to the shoreline. Deformation began in the Early Tertiary and lasted until the latest Miocene age. Structures in the southern part trend north-south, oblique to the shoreline, and there is evidence of compression.

Most of the production from the onshore Santa Maria basin is from fractured shale reservoirs of middle Miocene and Pliocene age, and rocks of equivalent lithology may be anticipated offshore. However, there are only two areas in the offshore basin where the sediment thickness exceeds 3000 m (10,000 ft), and it is questionable whether the thermal regime was ever sufficient to effect petroleum generation in the other areas. On a positive note, the data from the stratigraphic test (OCS-CAL 78-164 No. 1) drilled at Point Conception indicated a high geothermal gradient and significant oil and gas shows. This test, although oil and gas were logged and organic matter is dominantly the oil generating type, failed to show any prospective reservoir rocks, suggesting that fractured Monterey shale may be a reservoir target; oil is produced from fractured Monterey shale on the offshore part of the Santa Maria Basin.

The Outer Santa Cruz basin has basement rocks that are believed to be Franciscan. Cretaceous and lower Tertiary marine sandstones are present but have been subjected to deformation and erosion. Deposition of thick Middle Miocene cherty shales (Monterey equivalent?) was brought to an end in Late Miocene time by deformation and erosions. Subsequent sedimentation was characterized by fine silts and clays.

Tar-impregnated Middle Miocene cherty shales are probably source rocks. Older rocks are believed to have little hydrocarbon potential. Upper Miocene and Pliocene rocks have little reservoir potential, indicating that fracture porosity may hold the only reservoir potential.

The Bodega basin is underlain by Salinian granites of Cretaceous age. Thin Cretaceous Eocene sediments are scattered remnants of marine sandstones and shales. The Middle Miocene is characterized by cherty shales. This sequence was uplifted and eroded early in late Miocene time, after which marine clays and silts were deposited. Pre-Neogene complex structures of subduction tectonics were followed by the transition to strike-slip faulting, resulting in right lateral shear and folding parallel to the basin.

Pre-Miocene rocks are not very favorable for forming substantial petroleum reservoirs because of poor porosity and little onland production from equivalent strata. Tar and oil shows indicate the middle Miocene cherty shale may be a suitable source rock, and lower Miocene and lower Pliocene sands would make suitable reservoirs. Despite these favorable signs, the eight holes drilled on all the major structures have been dry.

The Point Arena basin has a basement believed to be pre-Cretaceous metasedimentary rocks. Onshore to the south, thick Cretaceous marine shales, siltstones, and sandstones crop out, but, like the Eocene clastic rocks, they thin rapidly to the north. Thick discontinuous basal sandstones of early Miocene age mark the beginning of a major episode of marine sedimentation. The middle Miocene is characterized by the cherty shales found in all the basins to the south. The upper Miocene sequence is represented by thick siltstones and claystones that grade upwards into Pliocene marine sandstones. Neogene deformation is most complex in the south end of the basin where there are major high-angle reverse faults and folds of Pliocene age that parallel the elongation of the basin.

Prospects for source rocks or reservoir rocks in the pre-Neogene section are poor. Outcrops on land show no potential source rocks; and the Eocene sandstones, which are dense, thin rapidly towards the basin. As in the basins to the south, oil shows are common in the middle and upper Miocene shales, which are considered potential source beds.

Lower Miocene and Pliocene sandstones are the most prospective reservoirs, but three wells located on major folds in the southeastern end of the basin were dry.

The Eel River basin offshore trends parallel to the coast and swings easterly in the south, where it extends onshore. The basement rocks offshore consist partly of the coastal belt of the Franciscan Complex of Late Jurassic to Eocene age and partly of the coeval "Yager Formation" of Eocene age. The coastal belt consists primarily of slightly metamorphosed, interbedded, fine to coarse grained clastic rocks. The "Yager Formation" consists of as much as 3000 m of marine shale, mudstone, siltstone, greywacke, and conglomerate. A very thin upper Miocene sequence unconformably overlies Eocene rocks. The Miocene through Pleistocene sequence, called, in part, the Wildcat Group, consists of over 3000 m of fine to coarse marine clastic rocks, representing a major later Miocene transgression accompanied by deepening of the basins in Miocene and Pliocene, and a course clastic sequence, representing a regression in the Pleistocene.

Major structures offshore are broad, predominantly symmetrical folds in Pliocene and younger strata, and they are aligned parallel to the axis of the basin. Some of these are piercement structures; others are associated with piercement structures.

The onshore extension of the basin, which represents only about 10% of the area of the entire basin, has produced some gas from the Pliocene section and only a trivial amount of oil from Upper Cretaceous sandstones and shales. The Miocene cherty shales, which are the probable source rocks to the south, are missing in this basin. All four wells drilled in the Eel River basin are dry. However, gasoline range hydrocarbons and gas were identified in a 1.6 m core recovered from the crest of a piercement structure west of Eureka. Reservoir quality marine sandstones within the Wildcat Group are fine grained and lenticular, and their distribution is variable. Eocene strata are represented only by scattered erosional remnants on the basement and are not considered to be good source beds or reservoirs.

OREGON-WASHINGTON

Oil (10^9 bbls)	Gas (tcf)
Mean	Mean
0.3	1.5

The continental margin off Oregon and Washington is a large sedimentary trough filled with Tertiary sediments overlying lower Eocene oceanic crust. The basin extends onshore to the western margin of the Cascade Range. Unlike the California margin, where the tectonic pattern is characterized by subduction and then transverse motion, the Oregon and Washington margin has been dominated by convergence or divergence between the Pacific (Farallon) and North American plates.

During early to middle late Eocene time, siltstones and sandstones that included turbidite sandstones were deposited in the deep water basin, while to the east thick clastic wedges marked shallow water shelf deposits. In late Middle Miocene time, a major period of underthrusting caused regional uplift in the coast ranges and on the continental shelf, and deposition of over 2500 m of upper Miocene and Pliocene sediments occurred in the newly forming basins on the Outer Continental Shelf.

Four such basins with sediment thicknesses that exceed 4550 m (15,000 ft) developed within the trough are the Willapa Basin on the north, and the Astoria, Newport, and Coos Bay basins to the south. Ten wells have been drilled offshore and three shallow holes have been drilled on state leases off Washington during the 1960s, as shown in Table 2-4, *Exploratory Test Well Data on Oregon-Washington Outer Continental Shelf.* No petroleum was produced from any of these wells.

Although thick sequences of organic-rich silts and muds of middle Eocene to Pliocene age were deposited offshore and in the adjacent onshore region, they are thermally immature. Exceptions are those located in the tectonically complex section along the west coast of the Olympic Peninsula. In addition to the area's unfavorable thermal history, its potential for suitable reservoir rocks is very low. Most of the clastic rocks penetrated in wells drilled on the OCS are fine-grained, and porosity and permeability in the sandstones is restricted by the presence of clay minerals and calcareous cement. In deformed strata, zeolites and silica have reduced the porosity significantly.

There are many major structures offshore including diapiric structures, some of which have been drilled already.

The core of the diapirs is a melange of sheared siltstone. The Astoria Basin probably has the greatest petroleum potential because it contains large anticlinal structures and thick Tertiary sediments that may have reservoir sands associated with Miocene delta-front fans

Table 2-4. Exploratory Test Well Data on Oregon-Washington Outer Continental Shelf.

NUMBER ON FIGURE 11	COMPANY AND NAME OF WELL	YEAR	LOCATION LATITUDE	LOCATION LONGITUDE	TOTAL DEPTH FT.	TERTIARY ROCKS PENETRATED	REMARKS
1	Pan America Well No. 1, P-0112	1967	43° 14.8'	124° 35.6'	6,146	Pliocene to early(?) Eocene	Bottomed in cemented sandstone
2	Union-Fulmar P-0130	1966	44° 3.6'	124° 38.8'	12,221	Pliocene to early Eocene	Bottomed in cemented sandstone
3	Shell Oil Well 1 ET-2 ET P-087	1965	44° 13.3'	124° 28.2'	8,353	Mio-Pliocene to early(?) Eocene	Bottomed in basalt
4	Union Oil-Grebe P-093	1966	44° 29.8'	124° 24.9'	10,010	Mio-Pliocene to middle(?) Eocene	
5	Standard Oil – Nautilus #1, P-0103	1965	44° 51.5'	124° 16.7'	12,628	Mio-Pliocene to late(?) Eocene	Hole bottomed in volcanic rocks
6	Shell Oil P-072 1 ET	1965–1966	46° 2.8'	124° 29.9'	8,219	Pliocene – (?)	
7	Shell Oil P-075 1 ET	1966	46° 9.1'	124° 24.5'	10,160	Pliocene(?) to middle Eocene(?)	Bottomed in basalt
8	Shell Oil and Pan Amer. P-0150	1966	46° 43.5'	124° 21.3'	13,179	Pliocene – lower Miocene(?)	Drilled on diapiric structure
9	Shell Oil 1ET P-0155	1967	46° 51.2'	124° 24.5'	11,162	Pliocene(?) – Miocene(?)	Drilled on diapiric structure
10	Pan American P-141	1967	47° 39.7'	124° 47.5'	10,368	Pliocene – Miocene(?)	

and fan channels. The Newport and Coos Bay basins also may contain reservoir sands associated with late Eocene deltas, but there are few large structures. The anticipated lack of reservoir sands in the western part of these basins and in the Willapa Basin place these areas at the low end of petroleum potential ranking.

GULF OF ALASKA

Oil (10^9 bbls)	Gas (tcf)
Mean	Mean
0.4	2.2

The continental margin of the Gulf of Alaska is composed of Precambrian to Middle Paleozoic rocks that coalesced with several northward moving microplates in the Middle Cretaceous age. In the Late Cretaceous age, a volcanic arc developed as a result of underthrusting by the Pacific oceanic crust. At the beginning of the Tertiary period, Pacific plate motion shifted relative to the Alaskan continental margin, resulting in the deposition of extensive deep sea fan deposits which later were accreted to the continental margin west of Kayak Island. They are strongly deformed, slightly metamorphosed, and locally intruded, and consequently they are not considered prospective.

This episode was replaced by regressive deposition in the Middle to Late Eocene age and by transgressive shales in the Oligocene and Miocene ages. The latter deposits from the Katalla, "Paul Creek," and Cenotaph Formations. From the middle Miocene period to the present, thick clastic sediments (Yakataga Formation) were deposited on a shallow shelf. A late phase of plate convergence resulted in complex structure in the Neogene rocks.

Despite the oil seeps and the discovery of one small oil field at Katalla, ten exploratory wells were drilled and abandoned; and one COST well was drilled short of its objective for technical reasons. Consequently, there is little data available on the presence and nature of source and reservoir rocks. Organic-rich samples of middle Tertiary age dredged from the continental slope are immature, but they may have reached maturity where they are deeply buried under the Yakutat shelf north of the Fairweather Ground.

Reservoir characteristics of sandstones dredged from the continental slope are poor. The rocks are compositionally and texturally immature. With the exception of a few outcrops of the Yakataga Formation, the sandstones have poor porosity and permeability because the interstices have been plugged by lithic fragments.

So far the results of drilling have not been encouraging for the western Gulf of Alaska despite its size, thick sediments, and abundant structures. The critical factor appears to be the lack of adequate reservoir sandstones in close association with middle Tertiary petroliferous mudstones and siltstones.

A greater potential appears to exist in the eastern Gulf of Alaska. Extensive dredging on the continental slope in the eastern Gulf of Alaska yielded an assemblage of rocks quite different from the three recovered onshore or in the Sale 39 area from the Yakutat Sea Valley to the Fairweather Ground. The oldest rocks recovered by dredging have been slightly metamorphosed argillites and sandstones, and they may be equivalent to the Yakutat Group of Late Jurassic to Late Cretaceous ages. These rocks are considered to be economic basement for petroleum in this area. Over 2800 m of Eocene or Paleocene organic-rich shales and siltstone with some intrusive rocks are basalt overlie this sequence; and they seem to be unconformably overlain by Oligocene silty shales containing abundant diatoms. The Oligocene unit may be equivalent in age to the "Paul Creek Formation" that crops out on land and has been penetrated by drilling in Sale 39. The Neogene strata are represented by a sequence of marine clastic rocks of widely varying lithologies.

The Paleocene rocks contain shales with high organic carbon contents suitable for source rocks. Organic geochemical analyses such as maximum pyrolysis yield, vitronite reflectants, and visual kerogen assessment suggest that the samples dredged from the slope east of Alsek Canyon and west of Yakutat Sea Valley are capable of generating oil.

The only rocks considered suitable as reservoirs are the Lower and Middle Tertiary sandstones. Dredging has yielded no rocks of younger age that have reservoir qualities.

In the absence of the large, young anticlines that were the dominant potential traps in the Sale 39 area, the best trap opportunities appear to be drape structures over basement relief and possibly structural-stratigraphic combinations in the Paleogene strata. In any case, traps will be subtle and more difficult to evaluate here than in the Sale 39 area.

KODIAK

Oil (10^9 bbls)	Gas (tcf)
Mean	Mean
0.4	2.0

There are three separate basins on the continental shelf south and east of Kodiak Island: the Tugidak basin to the south, the Albatross bank to the southeast, and Stevenson basin, the northernmost to the east of the island. The Tugidak basin contains up to five km of undeformed to moderately deformed upper Miocene and younger strata. The Tugidak uplift separates the Tugidak basin from the Albatross basin and forms the seaward edge of the Tugidak basin along the edge of the continental shelf.

The Albatross basin contains about five km of post-Upper Miocene sediment that, like those of the Tugidak basin, are only moderately deformed. The seaward edge of the basin is marked by the Albatross Bank, which has risen three km since the Late Miocene or Pliocene ages. The growth is recorded by a progressive shift in the depositional axis in the basin.

The Stevenson basin is separated from the Albatross Bank by the Dangerous Cape high. It consists of two small basins divided by the Portlock anticline. Sediment thickness in the southern basin does not exceed 3.5 km, but the northern basin contains as much as five to seven km of post-Upper Miocene sediment.

The onshore geology indicates that pre-Late Miocene time was characterized by volcanic activity. Late in the Paleogene, these rocks were exposed and truncated before subsidence in the Neogene. Onshore samples and those collected from coring at sea indicate that Paleogene sediments are poor source rocks — they are thermally immature and contain mostly herbaceous and coaly kerogen. If petroleum accumulations were in these rocks, they may have been destroyed during the late Paleogene erosion and truncation of structures.

Neogene reservoirs, therefore, are the most prospective but gas is the hydrocarbon most likely to be found.

LOWER COOK INLET

	Oil (10^9 bbls)	Gas (tcf)
	Mean	Mean
Total Cook Inlet	0.4	2.2

The lower Cook Inlet is part of a Mesozoic-Tertiary belt of sedimentary rocks that extend from upper Cook Inlet to the Shelikof Strait and the Alaska Peninsula. Marine Mesozoic rocks may be more than 10,800 m (35,600 ft) thick, and Cenozoic rocks may be as much as 7,600 m (24,000 ft) thick.

Rocks of the Early Jurassic age or older do not have petroleum potential and are considered economic basement. Middle and Upper Jurassic marine sedimentary rocks, Chinitna and Naknek Formations, unconformably overlie the basement sequence and are thought to be source rocks for the oil being produced in upper Cook Inlet. However, they are poor reservoirs.

Lower Cretaceous rocks unconformably overlie the Jurassic sequence and consist of siltstones and sandstones. There is no evidence that these rocks are potential source rocks, but the sandstone has fair reservoir characteristics. Upper Cretaceous rocks consist of a similar sequence of clastic deposits including shale; and, although no potential source rocks are known, the sandstone has good reservoir properties.

Tertiary rocks are all nonmarine, coarse, clastic deposits, including volcano clastic conglomerate. Some of these strata are potential source rocks for gas only. The conglomeratic sandstone has good to excellent reservoir properties.

Commercial oil production in upper Cook Inlet is restricted to the Tertiary sequence: 80 percent is produced from the Hemlock Conglomerate; 18 percent from the Tyonek Formation; and two percent from the West Foreland Formation. Similar geologic features in lower Cook Inlet have not yet proved so productive. Eight exploratory wells have been drilled, but only two had oil shows, neither of commercial quantities.

Initial enthusiasm for the lower Cook Inlet has waned. No drilling has taken place since June 1980, and no further plans have been announced to drill additional wells.

BRISTOL BAY BASIN

Oil (10^9 bbls)	Gas (tcf)
Mean	Mean
0.2	1.0

The Bristol Bay Basin shown in Figure 2-21 underlies the northern side of the Alaskan peninsula and extends offshore beneath Bristol Bay. The sediment thickness is greatest, about seven km, around Port Moller. The basin extends seaward as a great structural depression, not as a graben like the St. George Basin. Seismic reflection sections across the Amak Basin, the Black Hills Ridge, and the Bristol Bay Basin show that the acoustic basement is not clearly delineated as a strong reflecting horizon. However, there is a strong reflector representing an unconformable surface in the Amak Basin, over the Black Hills Ridge, and over the southern part of the Bristol Bay Basin. There is no direct evidence available on the age of the unconformity, but middle Cretaceous rocks are missing on the Alaskan peninsula, suggesting that the submarine unconformity might be of the same age. If so, then the sequence underlying the unconformity is a thick Mesozoic sedimentary section that represents initial basin filling. The flat overlying strata of Cenozoic and possibly the last Mesozoic age represent the latest episode of subsidence and sedimentation. The total sediment thickness in the Bristol Bay Basin, including the Mesozoic section, barely reaches 7 km, of which almost 3 km is a post-unconformity deposition.

No wells have been drilled in the offshore part of the Bristol Bay Basin. But nine wells have been drilled along the northern coastal region of the Alaska peninsula, which is shown in Map 2-1, *Alaska Peninsula Index Map.* No significant oil shows were reported in the four most northerly wells, but in the southern wells oil and gas shows were reported in the Miocene Bear Lake Formation, Oligocene "Stepovak Formation," and Eocene Tolstoi Formation. These shows

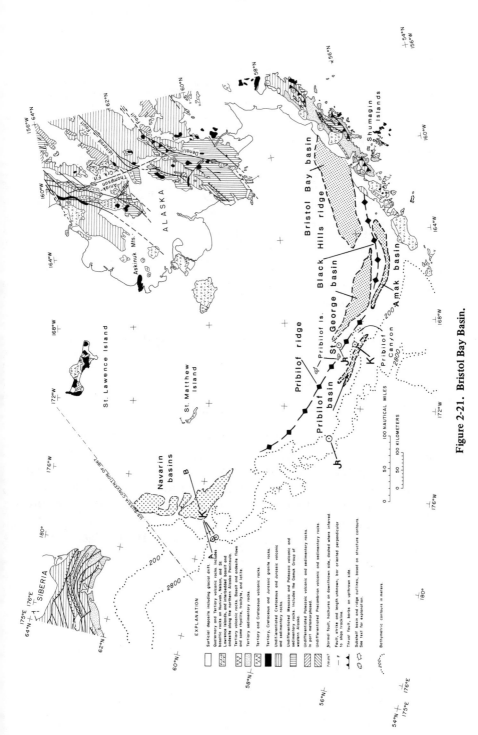

Figure 2-21. Bristol Bay Basin.

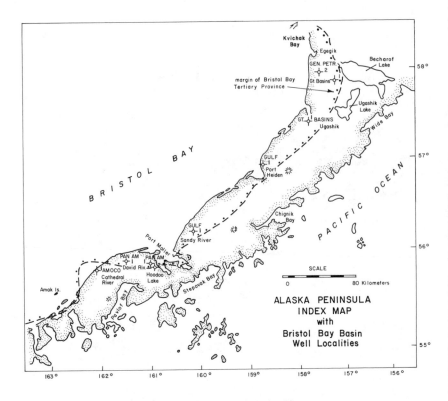

Map 2-1. Alaska Peninsula Index Map.

of oil demonstrate that at least locally conditions are favorable for petroleum formation. This is an encouraging sign for offshore hydrocarbons, considering the thick Cenozoic section offshore, but, in the absence of samples, a restrained enthusiasm would be prudent.

No major anticlinal structures have been identified in the offshore basin. The most promising structures lie along the uplifted sediments adjacent to the Alaska peninsula and the Black Hills Ridge. Farther offshore, sediments may be draped over deeply buried structures.

ST. GEORGE BASIN

Oil (10^9 bbls)	Gas (tcf)
Mean	Mean
0.4	2.3

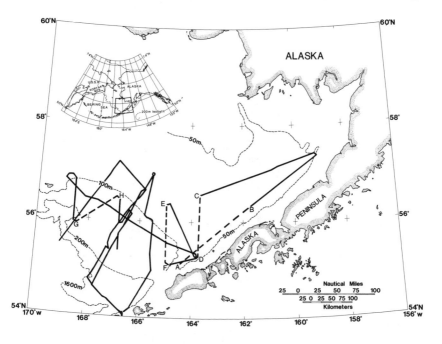

Map 2-2. St. George Basin (Marlow et al., 1979).

The St. George basin, shown in Map 2-2, is a deep graben formed by extensional rafting and regional subsidence of Mesozoic sedimentary rocks. Over 10 km of Cenozoic and possibly Upper Mesozoic sediment has filled the depression. Figure 2-22, *Seismic Reflection Profile of St. George Basin,* is an interpretative drawing showing prominent sedimentary reflective horizons on the shallow acoustic basement and in the deepest part of the basin. Reflectors noted below acoustic basement suggest the presence of folded sedimentary beds beveled off by Late Mesozoic erosion. Reflectors in the deeper part of the sedimentary section pinch out against the walls of the graben and are cut by normal faults that dip towards the basin axes.

The only well information in the St. George basin is from one COST well, but the data are proprietary. Therefore, the only available information on possible resource beds or reservoir rocks is from meager dredge haul samples scraped from the continental slope south of the basin and from inference and extrapolation from wells drilled on the Alaskan Peninsula. Mesozoic and Cenozoio rocks recovered by

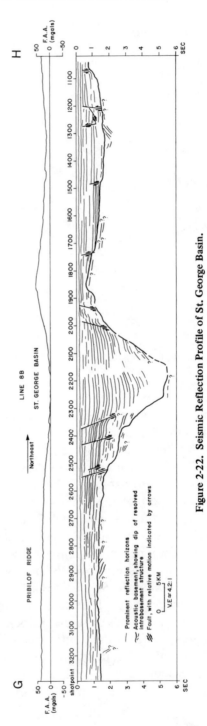

Figure 2-22. Seismic Reflection Profile of St. George Basin.

dredging contain very low amounts of organic carbon, commonly less than 0.27 percent. However, these samples are hardly representative of the section.

Data from wells drilled on the Alaskan Peninsula indicate that the best source rocks are marine shales and siltstones of the Oligocene "Stepovak Formation." Shows of oil and gas have been reported from the "Stepovak Formation" in three of the wells. Basal marine shales and siltstones of the Miocene Bear Lake Formation may also be potential source rocks. Lyle, et al. (1979) studied the potential Tertiary source rocks and concluded that dry gas would be the most likely hydrocarbon generated from them.

The Miocene Bear Lake sandstones are the best reservoir rocks on the Peninsula and probably have the greatest reservoir potential in the St. George basin. Shows of oil and gas have been reported in the Bear Lake lithic sandstones from two of the Peninsula wells. Older Tertiary rocks are dense, highly indurated, and exhibit poor reservoir characteristics.

Target structures include broad anticlines and growth faults along the margin of the graben. Potential stratigraphic traps may be present where the older beds thin and edge out against the flank of the basin.

NAVARIN BASIN

Oil (10^9 bbls)	Gas (tcf)
Mean	Mean
0.9	5.6

The Navarin Basin province shown in Figure 2-23 comprises three sediment filled basins that trend to the northwest parallel to the shelf edge. The southernmost basin is a large elongated trough, 200 km (125 miles) long, that contains more than 11 km of Cenozoic and possibly Mesozoic sediment. The central basin is the smallest of the three basins, 370,000 acres, and is filled with more than 10 km of sediment. The northernmost basin is the largest basin, covering 2.5 million acres, and it is filled with 12–15 km of sediment. Part of the western end of the basin extends west of the U.S.-Russia Convention Line of 1867. Anticlinal structures 10–15 km across have been identified near this convention line.

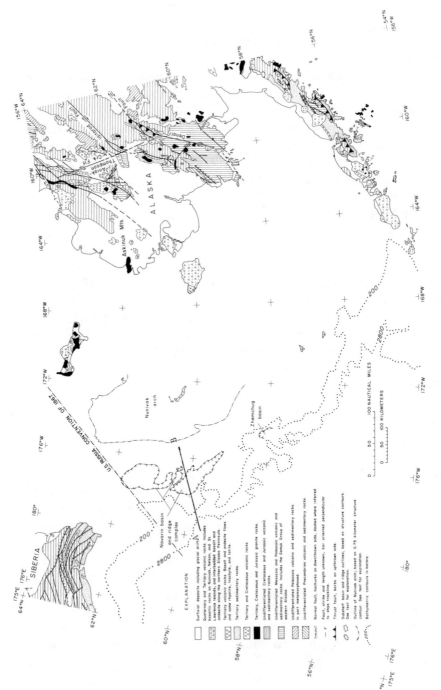

Figure 2-23. The Navarin Basin on South Bering Shelf.

Little is known about the geologic history of the Navarin Basin province because of the lack of samples. The acoustic basement is exposed on the continental slope south of the basins where it was sampled by dredging. The samples are Upper Jurassic or Lower Cretaceous volcanic sandstone and Upper Cretaceous mudstone. The reflectors at the outcrop can be traced northward beneath the thick sedimentary fill but cannot be identified beneath the thickest part of the section. Where the acoustic basement forms ridges, it appears to have been beveled into a wave-cut terrace. These samples suggest that the earliest sediments filling the basins may be of late Mesozoic age.

In addition to the Mesozoic rocks dredged from the continental slope, Tertiary mudstones and siltstones have also been recovered. Pyrolytic analysis of all the rocks indicate that, with the possible exception of one Cretaceous and one Jurassic sample, they are poor source rocks for petroleum. However, it should be recognized that dredging favors the sampling of the harder outcropping strata and may not be representative of softer strata that might escape the dredge.

Major anticlinal structures, which may hve diapiric cores, are potential structural traps that will attract early exploration efforts. Normal growth faults have been identified on the flanks of the central and southern basins. Deeply buried drape structures have formed where sediments overlie basement blocks that have been offset by several thousand meters.

Despite the lack of information on source and reservoir rocks, the massive volume of sediment and the presence of large structures make the overall prospects for the Navarin Basin province most attractive, perhaps more attractive than the U.S. Geological Survey assessments would indicate.

NORTON BASIN

Oil (10^9 bbls)	Gas (tcf)
Mean	Mean
0.2	1.2

The pre-Tertiary basement rocks include three distinct geological belts: a sequence of Precambrian, Paleozoic, and lower Mesozoic nonvolcanic sedimentary rocks, a volcanic belt, and a forearc belt that includes Mesozoic strata. Both the Norton and Hope Basins are Cenozoic features superimposed on these belts.

The oldest sediments over the economic basement are probably of Late Cretaceous age. This age is estimated, based on the concept that the Norton Basin formed as a tensional pull-apart feature associated with movement along the seaward extension of the Kaltag. The basin is characterized by a series of striking normal faults, West-Northwest, shown in Figure 2-24, *Structure Contours of the Norton Basin,* which break the basin into a complex of grabens and horsts. Some of these grabens may be as much as 7 km deep. From geological inference it can be postulated that pre-Late Miocene sedimentation may be nonmarine; a Late Miocene transgression marked a shift to marine sedimentation.

The petroleum potential of Norton Basin must be inferred from geophysical data and from onshore data. Middle Cretaceous deltaic and Tertiary nonmarine strata around the basin are generally gas prone, and it is inferred that the coeval sediments in the basin are

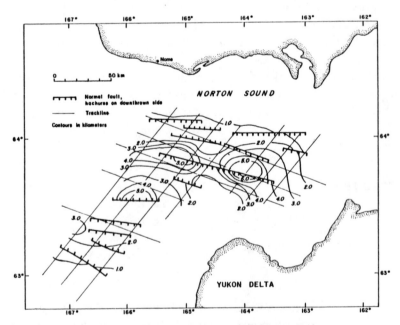

Figure 2-24. Structure Contours of the Norton Basin.

also gas prone. Some of the strata in the offshore are sufficiently mature to produce gasoline-range hydrocarbons as indicated by the analysis of samples taken from a gas seep south of Nome. The dominant gas emanating from the seep was carbon dioxide and the carbon isotope ratio of about –3 per mil PDB (Peedee Belemnite) standard indicate that it formed from the decomposition of marine carbonate rocks at depth. It is possible that the Paleozoic rocks buried beneath the Cenozoic may be a source of hydrocarbons. Although the samples collected from outcrops on St. Lawrence Island are immature, their equivalents could have reached maturity under burial.

If reservoir quality can be roughly related to the quartz content of the drainage area, the pre-late Miocene drainage of the Yukon River may have been greatly restricted and low in quartz. The post-late Miocene saw a major extension of the drainage area, and modern Yukon sediment contains an average of 25% quartz.

HOPE AND CHUKCHI BASIN

	Oil (10^9 bbls)	Gas (tcf)
	Mean	Mean
Hope basin	Negl.	0.3
Chukchi basin	1.4	6.4

The Hope Basin, shown in Figure 2-25 lies beneath the Chukchi Sea. It is a broad Cenozoic basin extending to the north of the Seward Peninsula, south of the Lisburne Peninsula and northwestward to west of the U.S.-U.S.S.R. Convention Line of 1867. West of Cape Lisburne the Hope Basin is bounded on the north by the Herald Arch, which separates it from the Chukchi Basin shown in Figure 2-26.

The Northwest orientation of the Hope Basin and its structures parallel the trench of the Herald Arch and are oblique to the trend of the Brooks Range.

The Hope Basin was formed by subsidence of Lower Cretaceous and older rocks of the Brooks Range and by a relatively thick accumulation of Cenozoic and possibly Upper Cretaceous sediments. The Cenozoic sediments barely exceed 3000 m (10,000 ft). The axis of sedimentation has shifted northward with time. Based on inference

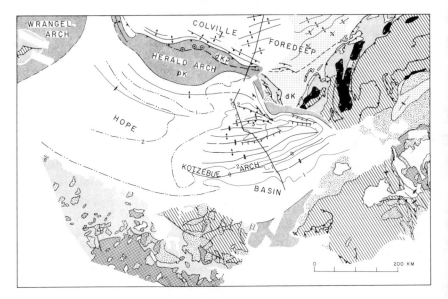

Figure 2-25. The Hope Basin (Chukchi Sea).

from onshore geology, the sediments in the basin may be predominantly nonmarine. The more recent sediments of Neogene age are probably marine.

East-West trending anticlinal structures are restricted to the southeastern part of the basin. Although most folding and faulting affect only the deeper strata, the dominant structure, the Kotzebue anticline, appears to have been active during the later stages of basin infill.

In terms of petroleum potential, the thickness of sediment is marginal for petroleum generation. Two wells have been drilled on the east and west sides of Kotzebue Sound, and the entire section drilled was reported as nonmarine. Since at least the earlier sedimentation in the basin is probably nonmarine, the likelihood of there being significant source beds buried at depths is not great. Reservoir rocks may be abundant in the basin based on the presence of abundant sands and conglomerates in the Kotzebue wells.

The Chukchi basin may be divided into two subbasins: the North Chukchi and the Central Chukchi or Colville Foredeep. The North Chukchi subbasin lies between the Barrow Arch on the south and east and the Chukchi Continental Borderland on the north. Its extent to the west is unknown. The subbasin contains a thick (greater

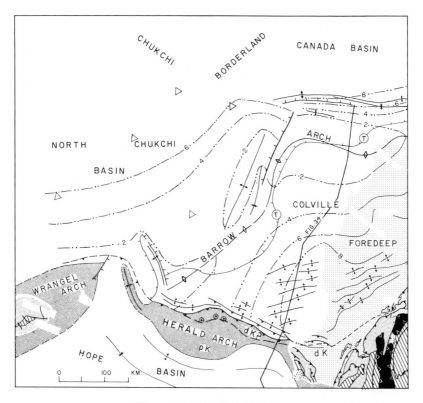

Figure 2-26. The Chukchi Basin.

than 6,000 m or 20,000 ft) sequence of clastic rocks of the Brookian (Upper Jurassic to Halocene sequence). Both marine and nonmarine beds occur in the coeval strata in northwest Alaska, but those in the basin may be dominantly marine. There are four major sedimentary units apparent on the single channel seismic records, and, based on sonobuoy refraction velocities and correlations with onshore units, these are probably Neogene, Paleogene, Cretaceous, and pre-Cretaceous.

Diapiric structures reportedly pierce Tertiary strata to within a few meters of the seafloor, and, based on seismic, magnetic, gravity, and regional stratigraphic data, they probably consist of shale. Based on the survey line spacing, there may be as many as 30 or 40 such structures.

The sediments in the basin are clearly thick enough to be of economic importance. Unlike those in the Hope Basin, these sediments are believed to be mainly marine. In the absence of wells in the area, nothing can be said concerning the presence of possible source rocks in the basin.

The Barrow Arch, associated unconformities, faults, and a major anticline that lies parallel and to the west of the arch represent major potential petroleum traps in the eastern part of the Basin, shown in Figure 2-26.

Bedded Ellesmerian (Mississippian to Jurassic) and Brookian rocks of northern Alaska trend beneath the Chukchi Sea and can be traced on seismic records south to the Herald Arch and west where they thin toward the Barrow Arch. All or part of the Ellesmerian sequence thins northward toward the Barrow Arch where it appears to pinch out on deformed lower Ellesmerian or Franklinian (pre-Mississippian) rocks. North of the Arch, Cretaceous strata are believed to overlie Ellesmerian-Franklinian sequences.

The Brookian rocks in northwestern Alaska are deltaic deposits, including both marine (delta front foreset) and nonmarine (topset) beds containing coal. This sequence can be identified on the seismic records in the basin with reasonable certainty. The deltaic environment may be favorable for the deposition of potential source rocks.

The structure in the southern part of the basin appears to be an extension of the Arctic Foothills thrust fault system. Broad east-west striking anticlines in the northern part of the fault system become tighter and have greater amplitude to the south where thrust faulting and incipient core diapirism is evident. Detachment folds appear to be of Late Cretaceous and early Tertiary age. Younger thrust-folds of the Herald Arch fault zone obliquely intersect the detachment folds of the Arctic Foothills thrust fault system.

BEAUFORT SHELF

Oil (10^9 bbls)	Gas (tcf)
Mean	Mean
7.8	39.3

The economic basement shown beneath the Beaufort Shelf in Figure 2-27, *Generalized Geologic Map of Northern Alaska and the Beaufort*

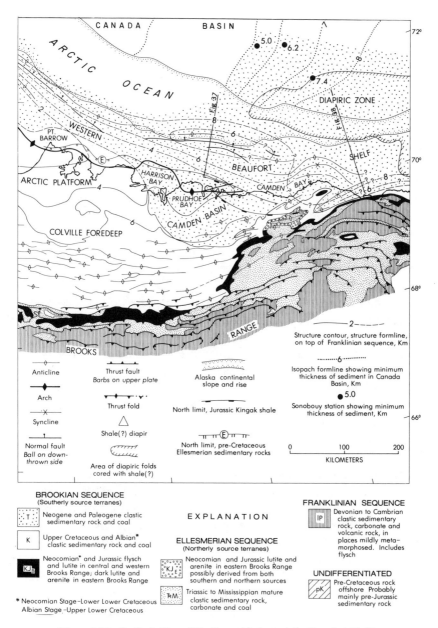

Figure 2-27. Geologic Map of Northern Alaska and the Beaufort Shelf.

Shelf, is the Franklinian sequence consisting of moderately to highly metamorphosed sedimentary and volcanic rocks varying in age from Cambrian to Devonian. After deformation and metamorphism, the top of the sequence was beveled into a broad platform called the Arctic Platform. The deposition of Mississippian marine sediments on the platform marked the initiation of the Ellesmerian sequence, a thick sequence of both marine and nonmarine clastic rocks that includes organic-rich shales. The source of the sediment was to the north, beneath the present Beaufort and Arctic Sea. The Ellesmerian deposition came to a close at about the time of continental rifting in the Arctic Sea in Late Jurassic and Early Cretaceous when the present continental margin was formed. Meanwhile, the southern part of the Arctic Platform subsided and was overridden by low angle thrust faults. The Colville geosyncline formed on the depressed Platform north of the mountains, which were uplifted at the time these nappes were emplaced.

Sedimentation from these mountains into the Colville geosyncline represented the initiation of the Brookian sequence. As the sediments filled the trough, they prograded northward over the inclined Arctic Platform, forming a time transgressive boundary with the waning northern Ellesmerian source area from the Middle or Upper Jurassic in the Brooks Range to the Lower Cretaceous beneath the Beaufort Shelf. Brookian strata onshore and offshore are mixed marine and nonmarine fine to coarse clastic rocks. Increased marine facies north of the Barrow Arch may be anticipated.

The Beaufort Shelf may be divided into two parts: the Barrow section, which includes the offshore area between Point Barrow to approximately long. 145° W., and the Barter Island sector, from long. 145° W. to the Canadian border. The southern part of the Barrow sector is dominated by the Barrow Arch which roughly parallels the present coastline. Franklinian rocks are overlain by Ellesmerian strata only in the southern part of the Barrow sector. Brookian rocks unconformably overlie both Ellesmerian rocks in the south and the Franklinian sequence in the north, where they constitute most of the sediments on the Beaufort Shelf. Onshore, the Cretaceous strata are mixed marine and nonmarine, and the Tertiary sequence is nonmarine; both appear to become marine, or partly so, offshore. The total thickness exceeds 6,000 m (19,800 ft) on the outer shelf.

Structures on the inner and central part of the shelf are restricted to normal faults and a broad fold on the outer part. The outermost shelf is characterized by rotational fault blocks bounded by normal faults, some of which are growth faults.

The Barter Island sector is underlain by Brookian strata overlying Franklinian rocks. The Ellesmerian sequence appears to be missing. The Tertiary rocks are predominantly nonmarine beneath the Arctic coastal plain, but probably become increasingly marine seaward. The Tertiary sequence may exceed 6,000 m offshore. The Barter sector is dominated by two anticlines and an intervening syncline that affected Upper Cenozoic rocks. The dimensions of these anticlines exceed 1 km amplitude, 10 km width, and 150 km length.

Both the Ellesmerian and Brookian sequences are demonstrably petroliferous. Of the thirteen major units of the Ellesmerian sequence, ten of them contain commercial or strong shows of oil or gas.

Within 10 km of the coast, there are a giant and a supergiant oil field (Kuparuk River and Prudhoe Bay), a small producing gas field (Barrow field), six undeveloped oil discoveries of unknown or unannounced economic potential, and several oil and gas seeps. Oil and gas have been reported in Brookian beds from the Flaxman Island and Point Thompson wells. To the east, Canadian exploration has resulted in the discovery of large accumulations of oil and gas in rocks that trend toward the Barter Island sector.

Chapter 3
Deepwater Drilling and Production Systems for the 1980s

J. Preston Mason

This chapter will briefly review the methods that will be used in the 1980s to develop hydrocarbon reserves found in deepwater locations and will examine the present and future capability of the oil industry, primarily the U.S. industry, to develop hydrocarbon reserves safely in deep water. There has been a long and orderly development program to develop that capability for production underseas, and an analysis of the state-of-the-art of various systems, with a qualitative indication of the applicability of each system, may be very useful.

There are two general areas of common misunderstanding about deepwater production systems. First, techniques and equipment, which will be examined here, are often heralded by the press as "new." In reality, these systems are the results of an orderly development program that has been active for many years. Second, perhaps contrary to popular belief, the oil and gas companies who survive in the industry are not so much innovative as conservative. They must take large financial risks by the basic uncertainty of searching for hydrocarbons usually located at great depths below the earth's surface. However, they also spend enormous sums of money to minimize the operating risks that could cause them to lose the hydrocarbons that are found. Many outsiders have argued that the public must be protected from the hazardous adventures of the industry by safety regulations of the government. While some regulation is not inappropriate, in reality the economic incentives for safety in the industry far outweigh the effects of public regulation. The following pages illustrate the enormous amount of time, effort, and money that have been spent in developing and providing the available deepwater production system.

In addition, it must be noted that there is no "best" production system for hydrocarbons in deep water. The circumstances of each hydrocarbon discovery determine which system is best for that specific use. This is the reason that oil companies frequently develop what appear to be competing systems. Each company develops the system that best fits its prospects as it sees them. In the end, each company will develop its discoveries using the best available system, regardless of who actually developed the system.

OVERALL CAPABILITY

Deepwater drilling and production systems have been developed by extending technology from land operations into ever increasing water depths. The progression has moved from land, to marshes, to protected shallow water, then to the open seas, and finally to hostile deepwater areas, such as offshore Canada.

The plot in Figure 3-1, *Deepwater Drilling and Production Capability,* presents the history of this development. The first offshore wells were drilled in the late 1940s. The first wells were drilled from bottom founded rigs that subsequently have been extended to water depths of about 350 ft, depending on soils and weather conditions. Floating drilling rigs, moored in place, were first used in the early 1950s. Drilling capability had moved to 600 ft by 1965.[1] With the award of leases in the Santa Barbara Channel in 1968, drilling experience quickly moved to 1,5000-ft water depth by 1970. The increased demand for oil led to a greater interest in deep water areas in the early 1970s, and exploratory drilling operations had moved to 2,500 ft of water offshore Australia by 1975. Interest in deep water has progressively continued, with drilling water depth moving to 3,400 ft offshore Surinam in 1976, about 4,400 ft offshore Africa in 1978, and about 4,900 ft offshore Canada in 1979.

Commercial production systems, moreover, have moved into deeper water following the exploration drilling. Fixed platforms were used in the late 1940s in water depth of 20 ft. Platforms were used in 100 ft by 1955, 200 ft by 1959, 340 ft in 1962, 373 ft by 1970, 850 ft in 1976, and finally 1,025 ft in 1978.[2]

The dashed lines in Figure 3-1 indicate my assessment of the progress of technical development. The basis for projecting the drilling

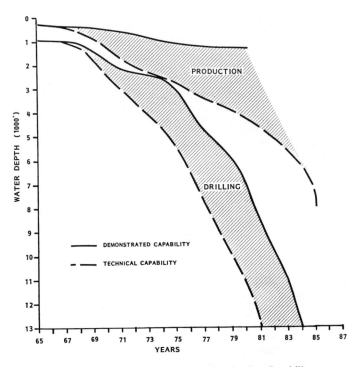

Figure 3-1. Deep Water Drilling and Production Capability.

capability is that currently available rigs are equipped to drill to 6,000-ft water depths. One drillship is reportedly being designed to drill in 9,000-ft water depths. In the National Science Foundation's Deep Sea Drilling Program, the *Glomar Challenger* has drilled in water depths to 20,000 ft to explore the geology of the earth's crust. That work in the deep ocean has been done without a riser or blowout preventer (BOP). In the next phase of that work, the Ocean Margin Drilling Program has planned to drill with a riser and BOP. That program, also sponsored by the National Science Foundation (NSF) and funded by NSF and several oil companies, has been developing capability and planning to convert the *Glomar Explorer* to drill in water depths to 13,000 ft in 1984.

As shown, drilling capability consisting of design capability and tested prototype equipment has preceded demonstrated capability by only a short time. Interest in exploration drilling has pushed technology in this area, and drilling capability has been used commercially almost as soon as the oil company management is convinced that the technology is safe. Production system availability has been based on prototype testing of diverless, deepwater, seafloor well systems, as detailed engineering and equipment development have been extending those systems.

Production technology normally lags behind drilling five to seven years. This is logical because drilling in frontier areas has traditionally required that long to define hydrocarbon reserves sufficiently to justify a start of commercial development of a field. Research resources are usually allocated to keep the lag in production technology within the five to seven year spread. The spread between capability and commercial use of production systems is an indication of the willingness of oil companies and manufacturers to initiate development of long lead technology in anticipation of deepwater discoveries and their expectation of availability of deepwater acreage. But the unusually long lag indicates the lack of success in the deepwater exploration up to 1981, largely due to the unavailability of deepwater acreage caused by political activities in several parts of the world, including the United States.

DRILLING SYSTEMS

The term "deepwater" used here means water depths of 600 ft and more. Thus, only floating drilling capability will be analyzed.

A general floating drilling system is shown schematically in Figure 3-2. A surface floating vessel, equipped with a drilling rig and the necessary support facilities, is stationed over the well site. The vessel can be held by a "mooring," ususally consisting of wire rope and chains, or "dynamically positioned" by computer controlled thrusters. The computers use position sensors to detect the position of the vessel relative to the hole and control the thrusters to keep the vessel within an acceptable excursion from the hole. A drilling riser extends between the surface vessel and the seafloor. This provides a conduit to guide the drill into the hole and a flow path for drilling mud used to control subsurface formation pressure and lubricate and clean the

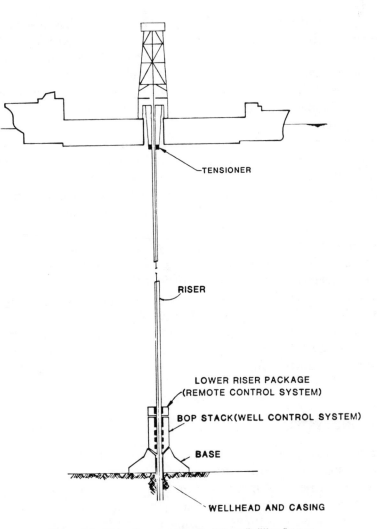

TENSIONER

RISER

LOWER RISER PACKAGE
(REMOTE CONTROL SYSTEM)

BOP STACK (WELL CONTROL SYSTEM)

BASE

WELLHEAD AND CASING

Figure 3-2. Major Components of a Subsea Drilling System.

hole. The riser is latched to a structural wellhead and base on the seafloor and held to an acceptable shape by tensioners mounted on the
vessel. A blowout preventer (BOP) is located at the base of the riser.
This unit is a set of remotely controlled valves capable of sealing around
the drillpipe or well casing, or shearing tubulars in an emergency.

For deepwater rigs, the BOP is operated by multiplex electrohydraulic control from the surface through an umbilical to control modules mounted on the riser base.

Ship-shaped drilling rigs are common. The ship shape provides ample space for the rig and supplies, lends itself well to dynamic positioning, and can be moved around the world easily and quickly. The *Discoverer Seven Seas,* for example, is a dynamically positioned rig that has drilled 14 wells in water depths from 362 ft to about 4,900 ft since November 1976. The 4,900 ft water depth well offshore Canada is the deepest to date.[3] This vessel is capable of drilling in 6,000-ft water depth.

Semisubmersible shaped rigs have been developed for use in rough weather areas. Improved motion behavior is gained at a loss of load capacity and mobility. The SEDCO 709 is the only dynamically positioned semisubmersible used today. It was used to drill a well offshore Canada in a water depth of 3,500 ft and in 1981 was operating in deep water in the North Sea. It can be equipped to drill in water depths of 6,000 ft and operate year-round with little downtime in areas such as the east coast of Canada. The 709 can also be reportedly modified to extend its capability to water depths of 8,000 ft.

As noted earlier, these floating drilling systems have been developed since the early 1950s. During each of the five years from 1975 to 1980, there were 60 to 70 exploratory wells drilled in water depths beyond 600 ft. In mid-1980, there were 112 drilling rigs designed and equipped to drill in water depths beyond 600 ft. As shown in Figure 3-3, 16 of these rigs were capable of drilling in water depths beyond 2,000 ft. Several additional rigs in 1981 were being built or equipped for deep water drilling.

PLATFORM WELL PRODUCTION SYSTEMS

Wells are drilled and completed above water whenever technically possible and economically feasible, and "fixed" structures are used where practical. However, where fixed structures, designed to withstand environmental forces, are not practical, compliant platforms that sway with large waves are used. And in deeper water, floating platforms will be used.

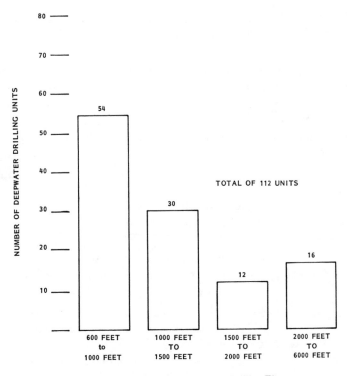

Figure 3-3. Capability of Deepwater Drilling Fleet.

Conventional Platforms

As noted earlier, conventional bottom-founded fixed platforms have been used since the mid-1940s. In this system, shown in Figure 3-4, the platform is built on shore, floated or barged to location, and installed on the seafloor. The decks are then installed. Drilling begins from the deck while production facilities are added. Production is started when the first wells are completed and the facilities are ready. When a market exists on shore, and the distance is not too far, oil and gas is taken to market by seafloor pipelines.* In deeper water, the oil is flowed through the pipelines to a single point mooring and loaded on tankers for transpor to market. When the oil is carried in

---

*Pipelines, single point mooring, and floating storage will be briefly discussed later in this chapter.

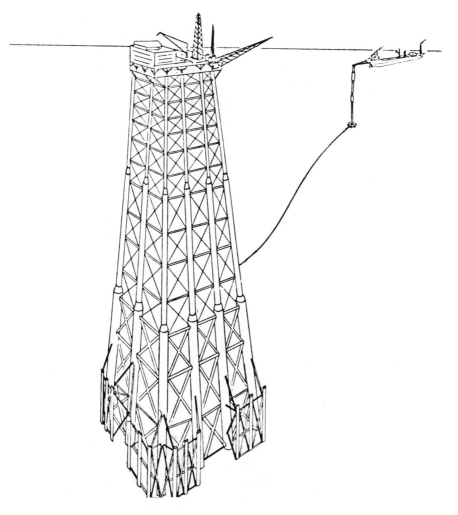

Figure 3-4. Conventional Platform Systems.

tankers, the gas is usually reinjected or burned. Oil storage can be provided in the platform base, or in a moored floating storage to smooth the operations when tankers are used.

The Cognac platform was installed in 1978 in the Gulf of Mexico to support 65 wells.[4] The Cognac platforms was installed in three sections which were mated underwater. Drilling is still underway.

The Cognac platform demonstrates that technology is available to design the fixed structures for both static and dynamic environmental forces. Methods for installation were also demonstrated. There is no doubt that even bigger platforms are technically feasible and could be built and installed; however, the cost is very high. It is generally accepted that with present oil prices and costs, conventional fixed platforms will not be economically attractive for water depths much beyond 1200–1500 ft.

Compliant Towers

The "guyed tower" is shown in Figure 3-5. A relatively slender structural column rests on the seafloor and is held upright by a spread mooring in the same manner as tall communication towers on land. The guy wires are cables which extend from the tower below the water line to clump weights on the seafloor and from there to mooring piles or anchors. In calm weather, the tower is held near vertical by the relatively taut mooring. In severe weather, the clump weights are picked up off the seafloor, the mooring becomes "softer" and the tower is allowed to sway up to two degrees with large waves.

Wells are drilled from the platform deck through conductors that penetrate the seafloor. The well conductors are designed to absorb the sway motions of the tower without damage.

Tests of this system, developed primarily by Exxon, were conducted in the Gulf of Mexico from 1975 to 1978. A 1/5 scale design of a 1,500-ft water depth was tested. Costs of this offshore test were shared by a number of companies. Results of the tests proved the design and verified the design procedures.[5] Designs have been made for several locations including one unit for use in 1,150-ft water depth in the North Sea. Exxon announced plans in 1981 to install the first commercial unit in about a 1,000-ft water depth in the Lena Field in the Mississippi Canyon Block 280 in the Gulf of Mexico during 1983.

The slender guyed tower being supported on the seafloor is more sensitive to deck load than conventional platforms, but is less sensitive than platforms supported by buoyancy. It can be used in water depths from about 600 ft to about 2,000 ft, depending on weather criteria. In deeper water depths, the structure would have to be much larger to withstand environmental forces or avoid dynamic motion, diminishing economic advantages.

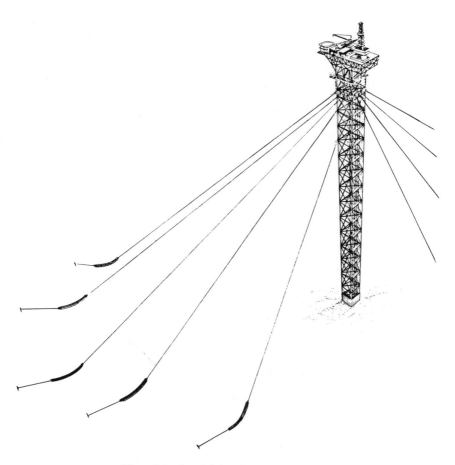

Figure 3-5. Guyed Tower Production System.

The "buoyant tower," shown in Figure 3-6, is also a relatively slender tower. It is anchored through a universal joint to the seafloor and held upright by buoyancy built into the tower. The more buoyancy that is built into the tower, the less the tower moves with the waves. There are, however, practical and economic limits on the amount of buoyancy that can be provided. Thus, the buoyant tower will probably sway more than a guyed tower. Wells will probably be drilled from the deck, but completed at the seafloor base and tied back through a flexible joint to the trees on the deck.[6]

No buoyant tower had been built up to 1982 to support production facilities. Elf installed an ocean prototype in 320 foot water

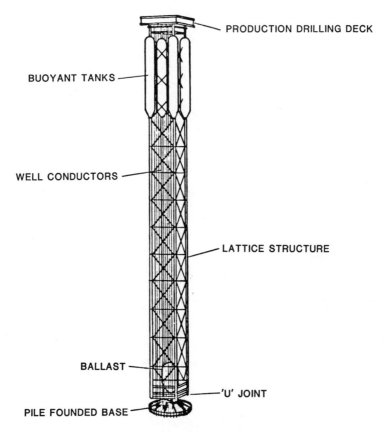

PRODUCTION DRILLING DECK

BUOYANT TANKS

WELL CONDUCTORS

LATTICE STRUCTURE

BALLAST

'U' JOINT

PILE FOUNDED BASE

Figure 3-6. Buoyant Drilling Production Tower.

depth in the Gulf of Gascogne offshore France in 1968. Since then, EMH, a French contractor, has installed flare towers in the Brent and Frigg Fields and shuttle tanker mooring in the Beryl Fields in the North Sea. The single anchor leg mooring (SALM) that was installed in 1981 to hold a large storage tanker in the Fulmar Field in the North Sea was also a form of a buoyant tower. Thus, while buoyant tower technology is not as advanced as guyed tower technology, the buoyant tower structure can be considered proven and available.

Design of the well completion and its tie-back as well as the flow-line connections for use with the buoyant tower have received much less attention than such designs for other types of platforms. Thus, additional development work is needed before a buoyant tower can be used as a production-processing platform.

The buoyant tower is much more sensitive to deck load, but, being in tension, it does not have the technical water depth limit of a guyed tower. Preliminary designs have been done for water depths to 3,000 ft. One study indicated that a deck load of 5,400 tons may be the economic limit for a water depth of 1,350 ft. For deeper depths, the allowable deck load will decrease.

Floating Platforms

Tension leg platform (TLP) is the generic term for floating, drilling, and/or production facilities that are anchored to the seafloor by means of highly tensioned, vertically aligned mooring legs (Figure 3-7). The floating platforms are typically steel structures configured much like a semisubmersible drilling rig. Vertical columns support the production decks safely above the splash zone and extend down to large underwater hull sections. Considerable buoyancy is required in the hull to adequately support the production equipment, in-process fluids, and the service facilities as well as to preload the risers and tension legs adequately.

Depending on the system concept, wells can be drilled and completed from the deck of the TLP, drilled and completed through seafloor templates beneath the TLP, or extended for completion on the platform deck. Production would flow directly from the wells or through a production riser from the seafloor wells to process facilities on the TLP. Oil would then flow down the risers to the seafloor pipeline to shore or to a separate oil storage and shipping terminal.

Up to 1982, no commercial TLP had been built to support production operations. However, a large amount of engineering development has been done. Development work to date has included a considerable amount of computer simulation of motion behavior and mooring forces. A number of model tests have been undertaken to build confidence as well as a data base for predicting TLP forces and motions. In addition, numerous preliminary designs have been done, and several of those designs have included detailed definition of system components. This work has resulted in a number of TLP configurations being developed.

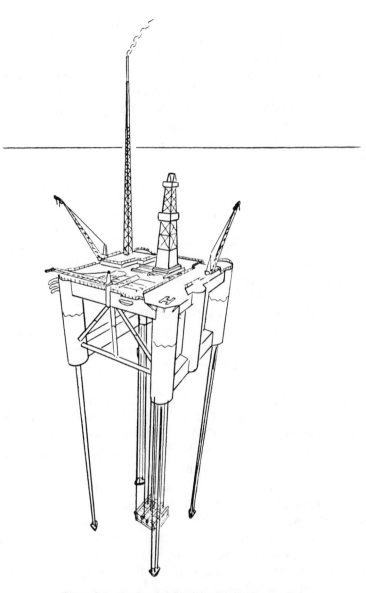

Figure 3-7. Tension Leg Platform Production System.

Deep Oil Technology (DOT) was one of the pioneers in development of the TLP. DOT's platform configuration was triangular with wire rope tension members extending down in three clusters to gravity anchors from each corner column. This system would utilize a centrally located, multiwell, subsea drilling template with either mudline suspension tie-back to the platform trees or a subsea completion. A 1/3 scale prototype of this unit was installed off California in the early 1970s.

Conoco announced in 1980 that a TLP would be used to develop the Hutton Field in the North Sea where the water depth is about 500 feet. A detailed design of that unit is in progress, and installation was scheduled for 1983.[7]

The TLP vessel is about the size or slightly larger than a large semi-submersible drilling rig. The system is sensitive to deck load and mooring forces which are related to weather criteria. The system is theoretically applicable to water depths from a few hundred feet to a few thousand, and some proponents feel the TLP could be used to 6,000-ft water depths.

SEAFLOOR WELL PRODUCTION SYSTEMS

Wells completed on the seafloor are drilled from floating drilling rigs and connected by flowlines to platforms or floating vessels. Seafloor wells are used to develop outlying areas of fields that cannot be fully developed by directional drilling from a platform, for locations beyond the water depth capability of platforms, and for fields too small to justify a full-sized platform or floating production facility.

Seafloor well technology has also been developing since the 1940s. However, development of equipment intended for use in deep water was started only in the mid-1950s. Figure 3-8 presents a plot of the number of seafloor wells versus years from 1960. The number of seafloor completions was less than 10 per year during the sixties and early seventies. Many of the early trees were diver installed and operated by hydraulic remote controls. Many were experimental. By the mid-1960s and later, more of the wells were equipped for electro-hydraulic control and many were considered commercial as opposed to experimental. In the mid-1970s the number of seafloor wells being installed increased. In 1979, there were 21 wells completed on the

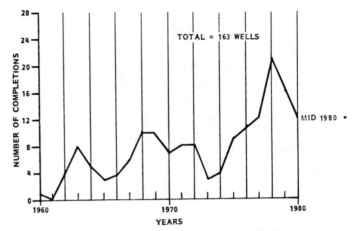

*ANOTHER 34 TREES WERE BUILT AND READY FOR INSTALLATION
AS OF JULY 1980.

SUBSEA WELLS INSTALLED PER YEAR

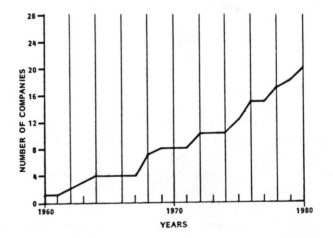

OIL COMPANIES INVOLVED SUBSEA
(CUMULATIVE)

Figure 3-8. Subsea Wells Installed and Companies Involved.

seafloor by nine oil operators. While the number of trees installed in 1980 appears to be less than previous years, this is not actually the case, as those shown are only for the first half of the year. Another 34 trees were completed and ready for installation at that time. Additionally, 34 trees were on order as of July 1980.

Another interesting trend is the number of companies that have had experience with seafloor wells. Figure 3-8 shows a plot of the cumulative number of companies that have installed at least one seafloor well. Corresponding to this trend is the list of manufacturers supplying subsea trees. They are:

Cameron	FMC/OCT
Lockheed	McEvoy
National	Regan
Vetco	WKM

Subsea well technology provides the capability to complete wells on the seafloor in virtually any water depth. The trees can be simple valve blocks equipped with hydraulic-actuated connectors, as shown in Figure 3-9. For more complex applications, a capability to use tools pumped from the surface into the well for downhole maintenance can also be incorporated. Flowline connection can be made by divers or it can be installed by remotely controlled tools. The control system can be a simple direct hydraulic control for one well, with one hydraulic control line per subsea valve, or it can be a multiplex electro-hydraulic system controlling many wells. Reliability techniques developed in the space program have been incorporated to provide remote controls that work for a long period without maintenance and can have backup controls that insure safety in the event of failure. The systems can be installed and maintained on guidelines, or guidelineless methods can be used.

Seafloor wells had been installed by 1982 only up to 600-ft water depths. However, they have been designed and installed using diverless methods, that makes their use possible in water depths up to several thousand feet.

SEMISUBMERSIBLE PRODUCTION SYSTEM

The system shown in Figure 3-10 consists of satellite wells connected by flowlines to seafloor base located directly under the semisubmersible.

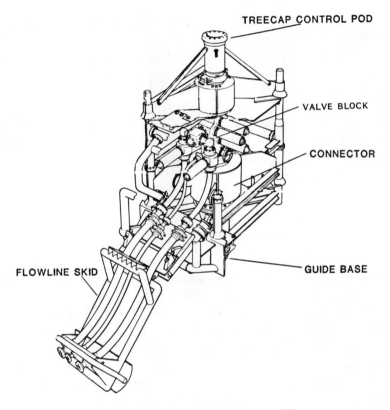

Figure 3-9. Cameron Plain Jane Tree No. TFL.

The semisubmersible would be a converted drilling rig or possibly a specially built vessel, kept on station by a conventional chain and wire rope spread mooring.

The production riser will carry fluids between the seafloor mainfold and the semisubmersible vessel. All seafloor equipment is controlled from the surface. Process and injection facilities will be located on the deck of the semisubmersible. Separated oil will be flowed down the riser through a seafloor pipeline. The pipeline could go to shore or to a single point mooring for a shuttle tanker for periodic transport to market. Produced gas would be used for fuel and put into a pipeline to shore, reinjected underground, or glared. Produced water would be cleaned and discharged overboard.

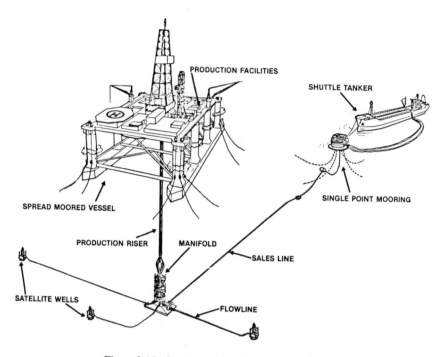

Figure 3-10. Semisubmersible Production System.

The system shown provides all the capability of platform systems and is applicable for small fields requiring few wells where no storage is justified. For larger fields requiring more wells, a seafloor manifold would be used to reduce the number of flowlines up the riser. A pipeline to shore or separate storage in the field would probably be justified to minimize the need to shut-in production. Use of the semi-submersible system would probably be limited to reserves that produce less than 100,000 barrels per day and to water depths of about 1,200 ft or less due to the limited deck load capability of drilling rig size vessels. Larger vessels would probably make this system less attractive than alternative systems.

Hamilton Brothers used the system to develop the Argyll Field in the North Sea, which was the first commercial use of the system for an entire field. Production was started in 1975, and the system has operated satisfactorily since that time.[8]

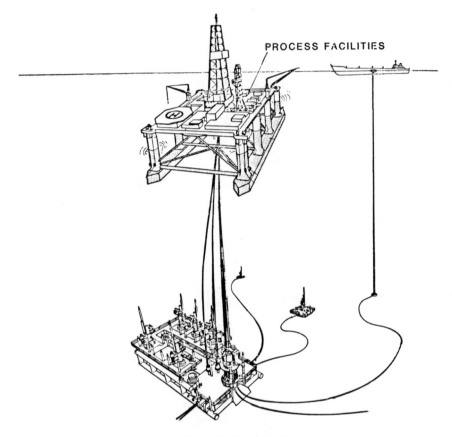

Figure 3-11. Petrobas-Enchova Field Development.

A variation of this system is shown in Figure 3-11. A multiwell template is located below the submersible. Wells are drilled through the template. Subsea trees are installed on the wells and connected to piping on the template which connects to the production riser. Satellite wells can also be drilled and connected to the template, as shown. This system is now being installed offshore Brazil.

One Atmosphere System

The one-atmospheric chamber production system is shown in Figure 3-12. Wells would be drilled in a conventional manner and completed with the trees inside a chamber kept at one atmosphere pressure. The wells would be connected by flowlines to manifolds, which would also be enclosed in a chamber at one atmosphere pressure. The manifolds are connected by pipelines to the base of a single point mooring production riser which transports the fluids between the seafloor and production facilities mounted on a tanker. All subsea equipment would be controlled from the surface. On board the tanker, oil would be separated, stabilized, and stored. The oil would then be transported to market by shuttle tankers that dock periodically with the storage tank. Gas would be recompressed and injected underground. Produced water would be treated and disposed of or combined with treated sea water and injected to maintain reservoir pressure.

If the field were near a market, the oil and gas would be transported by pipeline to shore. In that case, storage in the field would not be required and another type of vessel, but not a tanker, might be chosen to support process facilities.

Seafloor equipment maintenance would be done by men working in the chamber. The men and materials would be transported to site

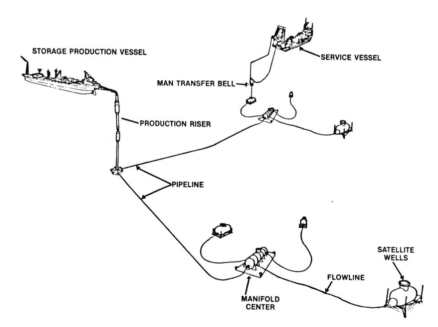

Figure 3-12. One Atmosphere Chamber Production System.

in a tethered manned transfer bell. The wells can be maintained by TFL servicing or by vertical reentry from a floating drilling rig.

Several enclosed seafloor wells and a prototype enclosed manifold have been installed during the last few years in the Gulf of Mexico by Shell Oil. That manifold was operated for about two years. The first complete field development system was installed in the Garoupa field offshore Brazil.[9] That system has been operating since 1978. Can-Ocean Resources, the successor to Lockheed Petroleum Services, has been operating two service vessels equipped to transport men to the seafloor chamber for maintenance.

Subsea Atmospheric Systems (SAS)

The production system shown in Figure 3-13 is a hybrid system developed by Mobil Oil. The wells are drilled through a base template and completed with special wet subsea trees. These trees are connected

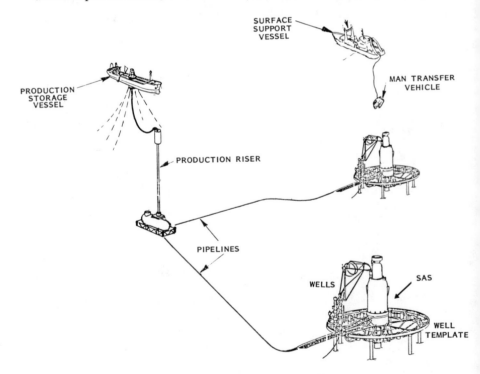

Figure 3-13. SAS Production System.

to manifolds and remote controls housed in a large chamber, which is installed on the base template. The atmosphere in the lower manifold section of the chamber is inert gas at one atmosphere pressure. A breathable air is maintained at one atmosphere in the upper control and entry section. Men are transported to the chamber in a tethered bell or submarine to do maintenance on the manifold and controls. The wells can be maintained by TFL servicing from inside the chamber or by vertical reentry methods from a floating drilling rig.

The SAS units are connected by pipeline to an enclosed atmospheric manifold center which also serves as a base for the production riser. The surface vessel supporting process facility is the turret-moored or dynamically positioned and connected to the top of the production riser by flexible pipe. The connection point is submerged below the wave zone. Pipes are also provided to supply nitrogen and air to the SAS. Power and communications are supplied by electric cable.

Work to develop this system began in the mid-1960s and led to the installation of a prototype of the SAS offshore in the Gulf of Mexico. Tests during 1972–1974 demonstrated the feasibility of the concept for water depths of 1,500 ft. The SAS has not yet been used commercially, although work to extend the system to deeper water has continued.

SUBSEA PRODUCTION SYSTEM (SPS)

The subsea production system developed by Exxon is shown in Figure 3-14. In this system, wells are drilled through a seafloor template. The wells are completed with special subsea trees that connect to a manifold circling the well bay area. The manifolds are connected to a production riser by pipeline. Production facilities are located onboard a floating production vessel. Seafloor equipment is controlled from the surface.

Wells are maintained by TFL servicing from the surface station or by vertical reentry from a floating drilling rig. Seafloor equipment is maintained by a special-purpose manipulator shown in Figure 3-15. The manipulator is operated from a surface vessel to land on a track on the seafloor template. The unmanned manipulator is then controlled from the surface to replace control modules or valves.

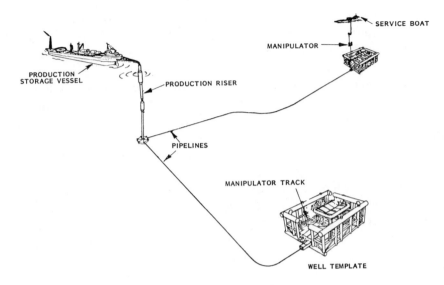

Figure 3-14. Subsea Production System (SPS).

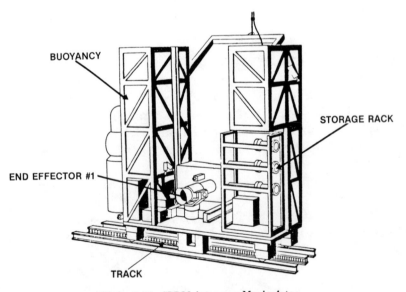

Figure 3-15. SPS Maintenance Manipulator.

Development of this system started in 1968 and concluded with the operation of a three-well prototype in the Gulf of Mexico during 1974 to 1978.[10] The test included the seafloor template, wells, diverless flowline and pipeline connections, and production riser. The maintenance manipulator was also fully tested. That test demonstrated capability of the SPS to water depths of 2,000 ft and beyond. A prototype of a deeper water version of the production riser was installed by Exxon in 1981 in the Santa Barbara Channel.

Technology developed in the SPS program has been combined with satellite well technology by Shell and Exxon for a commercial application in the Cormorant Field in the North Sea. A nine-well system

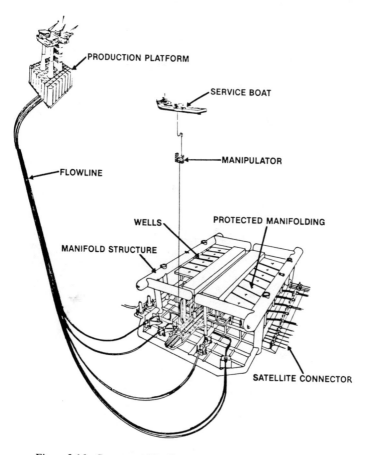

Figure 3-16. Cormorant Manifold Center Oil Production Center.

for that field, shown in Figure 3-16, was undergoing testing near Rotterdam, Netherlands for installation in 1982.

FLOWLINES AND PIPELINES

Installation of flowlines and pipelines can be done using a conventional lay barge, a reel barge, or a "tow" method. Flowlines and small-diameter pipelines can also be run vertical from a drilling rig and laid on the seafloor by moving the rig.

The conventional lay barge, shown in Figure 3-17 is actually a floating plant where pipe is brought onboard, welded to the line, inspected, fed off the back of the barge, and lowered to the seafloor. During laying operations, the pipe shape is controlled by holding tension in the pipe to avoid buckling at the seafloor and by use of a ramp (stinger) to control bending as the pipe leaves the vessel. Most existing barges are held in place by spread mooring systems and moved forward by moving the anchors. These barges are limited by their mooring system to water depths of about 1,000 ft. The pipe tensioners are capable of handling 20-inch pipe in water depths of 1,500 ft and smaller

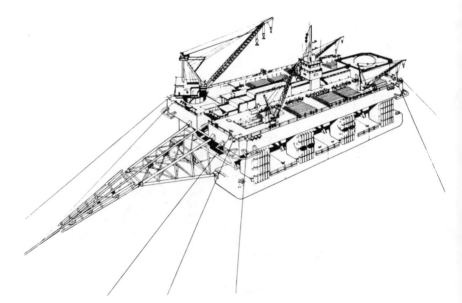

Figure 3-17. Semisubmersible Laybarge Semac 1.

Figure 3-18. Apache Pipe Laying Reel Ship.

size pipe in deeper water.[11] The *Castoro Sei* is also a semisubmersible lay barge. It is equipped to stay on station by spread mooring or dynamic positioning. The *Castoro Sei* recently laid three 20-inch pipes across the Mediterranean Sea in water depths up to 2,000 ft. The vessel reportedly maintained a rate of about 5,000 feet per day in all water depths. Calculations reportedly indicate that this vessel is capable of operating in water depths of 8,000 ft.[12]

A reel barge can lay pipe faster than a conventional barge. The *Apache,* shown in Figure 3-18 is a new dynamically positioned reel barge. In this approach, the pipe is welded and inspected on land and spooled onto a large reel onboard a barge. The barge then moves to the site and reels the pipe off. The shape of the pipe is controlled with tension as before, but the pipe leaves the barge in a vertical orientation so that a minimum-sized stinger is required. The laying operation is fast, which reduces the need to stay precisely on station for long periods and makes dynamic positioning of the barge practical. The *Apache* is capable of laying up to 16-inch pipe at speeds of reportedly two knots in water depths up to 3,000 ft. The vessel recently laid a 10-inch line in the Ninian field in the North Sea at a reported rate of 1,383 ft/hour.[13]

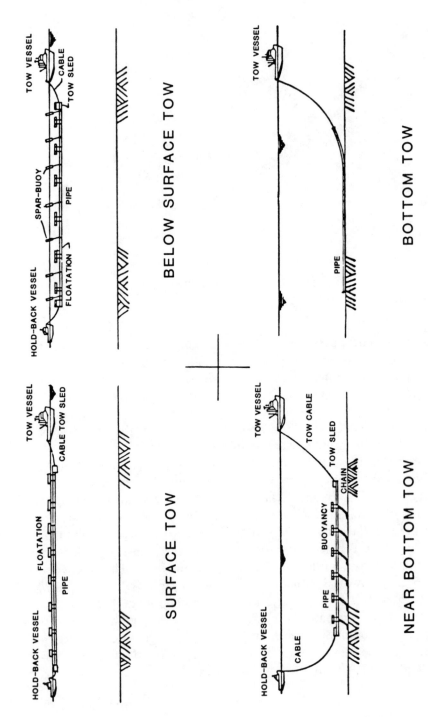

Figure 3-19. Flowline/Pipeline Tow Installation Methods.

Tow methods are shown in Figure 3-19. In this method the pipe is again made up and assembled on shore near the water. The pipe is then towed to the site either on the surface, or near the surface suspended from buoys, or on the bottom, or near the bottom kept by chains dragging along the seafloor. Pipe lengths for the tow to deepwater will probably be limited to about 10,000 ft to permit a reasonable use of two tugs and to allow control of the pipe. For longer lines, multiple tows will be required, and the ends will have to be docked and connected at the site.

Tow techniques have been used for many lines installed in shallow water. A near-bottom tow for the installation of satellite well flowline bundles was completed in 1980 in the Murchison Field in the North Sea. A near-surface tow system designed for deep water was tested by installation of a 2,000 ft satellite well flowline bundle in the Gulf of Mexico during 1980. A 2,000-ft section of 30-inch pipe was towed across the Norwegian Trench to prove the feasibility of the method.[14] Thus, although this method has not yet been used in deep water, it is feasible and design methods have been demonstrated.

Laying pipe from a drilling rig is slow. The pipe must be connected by mechanical connectors or welding while hung vertically in the derrick. (Screwed connectors for large-diameter lines have not been accepted for pipelines.) Pipe must also be brought to the rig in relatively small quantitites because of the limited onboard storage capability. A small stinger must be added to the rig to control the shape of the pipe when it leaves the rig during rig movements. This method has been considered in several instances and the design work has been done, but no significant lines had been installed from a drilling rig up to 1982.

The connection of pipelines in deep water must be done by remote controlled equipment. There are three steps. First, the pipe must be laid in the vicinity, then it must be aligned and positioned, then it can be connected and a seal made. The major technical problems are with positioning and aligning the pipe. Connectors are available to seal the pipe reliably by remote control once it is in place.

Connection of flowlines in deep water can be accomplished by upgrading the systems that have been developed. Diverless systems to connect flowlines or bundles of a few flowlines up to 6-inch in diameter have been developed by Cameron, Vetco, Regan, McEvoy, and FMC. Each of these systems involve laying the flowlines beside the connection point and pulling them in, using cables routed through sheaves on the base plate at the connection point. The Cameron, Vetco, and Regan systems can be used confidently in depths to 3,000 ft and beyond wherever guidelines and/or drawdown lines can be used.

In locations where only one end of the line needs to be on the sea-floor in deep water, existing, proven, vertical initiation methods can be used with conventional or reel barge installation methods. By this method, the pipe is lowered vertically on guidelines from a drilling rig and landed on the seafloor base. The line is then passed to a lay barge and laid away. The connecting system allows the pipe to pivot at the seafloor so that the line will lower from vertical to horizontal as the laying operation proceeds away from the connection point. The connection is made using tools lowered from the drilling rig. Cameron has equipment that has been used efficiently for vertical initiation pipe laying.

Connection of the larger lines in deeper water or where both ends are on the seafloor will require additional technical development. The Cameron and Regan systems for connecting flowlines can probably be scaled up to connect lines in the 10 to 12-inch range. Methods proposed for connecting larger lines use spool pieces, which are installed by using large, remotely controlled manipulators. These systems are only concepts and have not yet been proven.

SINGLE POINT TANKER MOORING SYSTEM

Concepts for mooring a shuttle or storage tanker are shown in Figure 3-20. Each of these systems can be used to moor a tanker permanently to provide storage in the field. The CALM and a SALM with hawser mooring can be used for temporarily mooring shuttle tankers. In general, the catenary chain system will be attractive for shallow water and calm weather areas. The structural riser will be better for deeper water and rougher weather locations.

Each of the concepts, with the exception of the turret and URI mooring, has been used commercially in many locations and are therefore proven. The largest unit is the SALM, which was being installed in 1981 in the Fulmar Field in the North Sea to moor a 200,000 dwt tanker permanently.

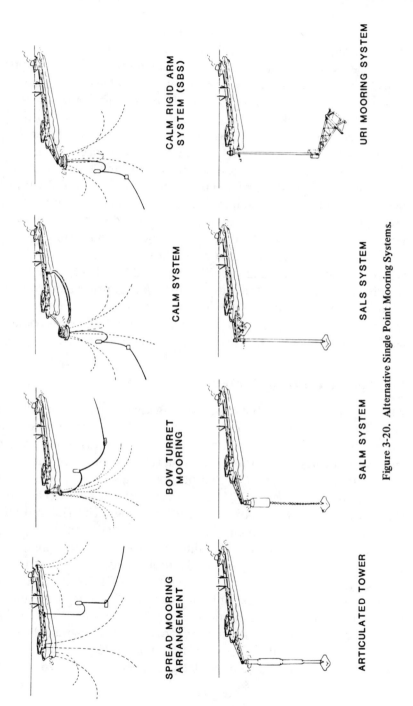

CALM RIGID ARM
SYSTEM (SBS)

URI MOORING SYSTEM

CALM SYSTEM

SALS SYSTEM

BOW TURRET
MOORING

SALM SYSTEM

SPREAD MOORING
ARRANGEMENT

ARTICULATED TOWER

Figure 3-20.   Alternative Single Point Mooring Systems.

The deepest water in which a system has been installed is about 500 ft. However, extensive research has been done to develop systems for deeper water. Such research has included sophisticated computer analysis and model testing. Preliminary designs have been made for Single Anchor Leg Mooring (SALM) type systems for water depths to 6,000 ft for tankers as large as 250,000 dwt and for North Sea weather conditions. Exxon has installed a prototype of their deep-water SALM in the Hondo Field in the Santa Barbara Channel. Based on the experience with shallow water systems and the development work that has been done on deeper water systems, coupled with the fact that a tanker storage and loading system could be located in shallow water away from the field, it can be assumed that technology for tanker mooring is available for deepwater production systems.

Dynamic positioning can also be used to hold a production-storage vessel on station. Dynamic positioning would probably be used for locations where the water depth, weather, ice, or other factors would make a permanent mooring either impractical or very expensive. The technology and equipment in use for deepwater drilling rigs could be used to control the larger thrusters that would be required.

MANNED MAINTENANCE SYSTEMS

Although the systems that have been described will be installed in deep water by diverless techniques, there will probably be occasions when manned subsea maintenance systems will be the most economical method for some of the installation steps or for the maintenance of the subsea equipment. For that purpose, manned manipulator systems, as shown in Figure 3-21, have been developed by Oceaneering Company as a backup to diverless running tools. The JIM system is a diving suit worn by a man. This unit is lowered from the surface and lands on decks built onto the subsea equipment. The suit is equipped with life support and special tools to allow a man to do pre-planned jobs. JIM can be used in water depths of 1,500 ft to untangle cables, operate hand valves, or attach cables. The latest template designed by VETCO for Petrobras (Figure 3-21) was designed so that JIM could be equipped with special tools for replacing failed valves. All life capability would be provided from the surface. Since the entire JIM system is transportable by air freight, it can be moved to site and

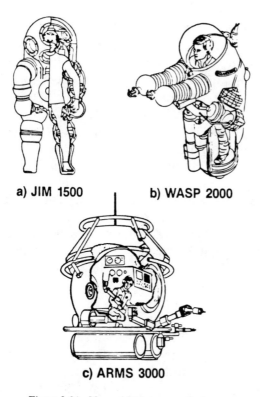

a) JIM 1500   b) WASP 2000

c) ARMS 3000

Figure 3-21. Manned Maintenance Systems.

set up in a few days. It can operate off any vessel capable of staying on location. Designs are available to extend the water depth capability of JIM to 3,000 ft, and development work is underway to extend the system to 4,500 ft and beyond. In summary, the JIM system provides slightly less dexterity and work capability than a saturation diver but without the long, expensive mobilization costs, and with greater water depth capability.

The WASP is a small swimming submersible worn by a man. This unit has about the same capability as JIM, except that it swims rather than walks, and the unit has been designed for use in 2,000-ft water depths. Development work is also being done to extend the operating capability of the WASP to much deeper water depths. Again, several special tasks can be performed by WASP. The tasks are probably more specialized than with JIM, but less preparation during design is required.

The ARMS system is a manned tethered bell equipped with a very sophisticated arm and a grabber arm. The unit is lowered to the sea-floor site and landed. The unit is equipped with an anchor and has some propulsion capability to allow the pilot to hover off the bottom to do his work. The arm includes shoulder, elbow, and wrist action and is equipped with position and force feedback. This means that the operator can place his hand in a control grip, move his hand, and actually feel the force being exerted by the arm. This allows the man in the bell to do rather sophisticated tasks, such as replacing a hydraulic hose or threading a nut onto a bolt. Existing ARMS bells are designed and proven for water depths of 3,000 ft. Designs have been made for depths of 4,500 ft, and the bell design could be extended to virtually any depth. A unit has actually been used in support of the Ben Ocean Lancer in 2,860-ft water depth.

SAFETY AND RELIABILITY

Each system has been designed to be safe, to protect the environment, the reserves, and the investment. During design, engineers have identified problems that could occur and have designed in reliability to avoid problems, with backup or redundant equipment or allow the system to "fail-safe" and to provide recovery from any failures.

The oil companies invested considerable money and manpower in each of these systems for about 10 years before they were ready for use. Only proven components have been used in offshore production systems, even more so than on land. The equipment is built big and heavy, and it is tested extensively before and during installation.

The systems have been designed to resist damage. Platforms and surface vessels have been designed to withstand 100-year storms without damage. Seafloor wells have been designed to withstand being caught and lifted by fishing gear or anchors from fishing boats or service boats. Template wells have been encased in massive structures that will withstand any dragged object and most dropped objects. Flowline connections have been designed to withstand the pulling of flowlines or pipelines without damage to the well or template structure.

CONCLUSION

The gas and oil industry, after some 20 years of technical developments, has the capability to exploit hydrocarbon resources beneath water several thousand feet deep. A number of companies have been engaged in this research and engineering, which has resulted in hardware components and procedures that can be used to form the production system that best meets the requirements of a specific field. These developments are not complete, for there are still many areas where improvements in equipment are needed. However, most of the future work for deepwater drilling and production systems will be aimed at improving efficiency and reducing costs rather than developing a basic capability.

NOTES TO CHAPTER 3

1. Witt, Robert R. Jr., "Exploring the Deeper Seas," *Offshore*, June 5, 1980, pp. 54–64.
2. Lee, Griff C., "Design of Platforms for Deep Water," *Offshore*, April 1978, p. 92–98.
3. Leonhardt, G.W., "Drilling in Record Water Depth was an Operational Success," *World Oil*, February 1, 1980, pp. 57–60.
4. Sterling, G.H., Cox, B.E., and Warrington, R.M., "Design of the Cognac Platform for 1025 Feet Water Depth, Gulf of Mexico," *OTC Proceedings 1979*, OTC Paper 3494.
5. Finn, L.D., "A New Deepwater Offshore Platform – The Guyed Tower," *OTC Proceedings 1976*, OTC Paper 2688; Finn, Lyle P., Wardell, John B., and Loftin, Thomas D., "The Guyed Tower as a Platform for Integrated Drilling and Producing Operations," *European Offshore Petroleum Conference and Exhibition*, Paper EUR 24, 1978; Fletcher, Sam, "Exxon Eyes Guyed Platform for '83," *The Houston Post*, February 11, 1980, pg. 14A.
6. Kennedy, John L., "Buoyant Tower Would Allow Deepwater Platform Drilling," *The Oil and Gas Journal*, October 28, 1974, pp. 60–64, 69–72; Alleaume, J. and Leturcq, M. "Articulated Column Designed for Production in Deep, Heavy Waters," *Ocean Resources,* September 1977, pp. 14–15, 18, 20, 23.
7. Ives, George O., "Tension Leg Platform Picked for Hutton Development," *Petroleum Engineer International*, March 15, 1980, pp. 22–28.
8. Hammett, P.S., Johnson, J.S. and White, J.L., "First Floating Production Facility – Argyll," *OTC Proceedings 1977*, OTC Paper 2821.
9. Burns, G.E. and D'Amorim, G.C., "Buoyant Towers for Phase 1 Development of Garoupa Field," *OTC Proceedings 1977*, OTC Paper 2828.

10. Robertson, Rob, "Exxon's Subsea Production System — Producing Oil/Gas by Remote Control," *Offshore*, October 1977, pp. 72–81.
11. "Semac Lays Pipeline in Record Speed," *Offshore*, February 1979, pp. 74–82.
12. Crawford, Diane, "Inclined Ramps Key to Deep Pipelaying," *Offshore*, May 1979, pp. 117–120.
13. Jorgensen, Svend, "Flowlines Laid by Reel-Ship Apache," *Oil and Gas Journal*, May 5, 1980, pp. 160–168.
14. *Ocean Industry*, December 1975, p. 30.

Chapter 4
Artic Drilling and Production Systems*

Hans O. Jahns

The five-year Outer Continental Shelf (OCS) lease schedule proposed in 1981 included an increased number of lease sales in Alaska's frontier areas. The petroleum industry has been prepared and ready to operate in this environment. Much of the technology required to drill and produce in ice covered waters is already in existence. Research and evaluation of new technology have been conducted in the past few years and will continue in the future to insure that the petroleum industry will have the ability to explore, develop, and produce in all Arctic areas in a safe and efficient manner. What is needed are lease sales and discoveries that will justify a commitment to actually design and construct the specialized equipment that will be needed to operate in these areas.

Before describing some of the existing and potential future technology for offshore Arctic drilling and production systems, some comment on the relevant factors of the physical environment on shelf areas to the north and west of Alaska may be helpful. Map 4-1 shows the Alaskan OCS with depth contours in meters. Most of the shelf to the west and north of Alaska is in relatively shallow water, typically lsss than 100 m deep. That is fortunate because ice forces are easier to resist in shallow water than in deep water. (It is harder to overturn a short structure than a tall one.) Water deeper than 100 m does occur near the edge of the shelf. The bank of intermediate water depth, 100 to 200 m, is relatively broad on the Bering Sea shelf, but quite narrow along the Beaufort Sea to the north. The southwestern

---

*Parts of the text of this chapter have been excerpted from an earlier paper by the author entitled "Arctic Platforms," which appeared in *Proceedings of a Symposium on Outer Continental Shelf Frontier Technology,* conducted by the Marine Board, Assembly of Engineering, National Research Council, National Academy of Sciences, Washington, D.C., 1980.

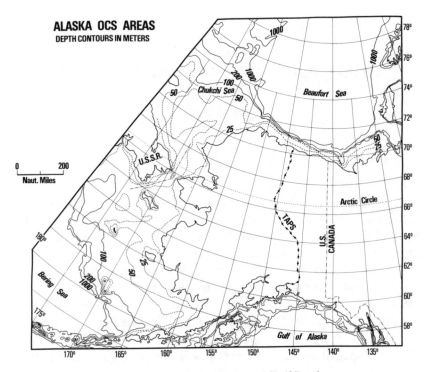

Map 4-1. Alaska Outer Continental Shelf Depths.

edge of the Bering Sea shelf experiences only marginal sea ice during a short period in winter, while the northern edge of the Beaufort Sea shelf is covered by thick Arctic pack ice virtually year-round.

Map 4-2 indicates the average and absolute maximum sea ice extent in winter, and the average and absolute minimum sea ice extent in summer on the Alaska Outer Continental Shelf. In any given year, one can expect little or no ice beyond the line of the average maximum sea ice extent. Conventional open-water drilling equipment can be used here with only minor interruptions due to sea ice. In the Beaufort Sea, one can expect little or no open water in a given year along the line of average minimum sea ice extent. For practical purposes, conventional floating drilling operations north of this line are ruled out.

Map 4-2 also includes some statistical data on the duration of the annual open-water season. This information is very important to the

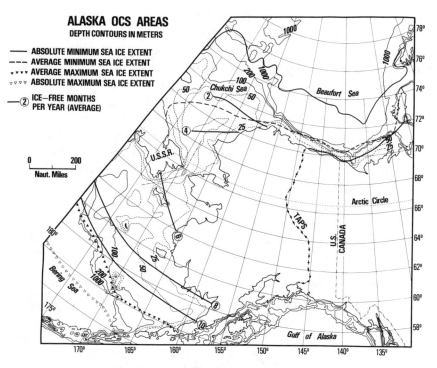

Map 4-2. Alaska Outer Continental Shelf Sea Ice Extent.

selection of drilling equipment, to the scheduling and cost of exploration drilling, and indeed, to the pace at which a given lease area can be explored. The circled numbers indicate the average length of the summer open water season, in months — ranging from two months in the northern Chukchi Sea to ten months in the southern Bering. Based on this data, one can broadly classify the entire shelf area into three zones: *First,* the Bering Sea, with generally more than five months open water. Conventional open-water drilling systems can be used on a seasonal basis for exploration drilling in this area, without incurring too great a penalty in cost and time. *Second,* the southern Chukchi Sea, with two to five months of open water, is a zone where conventional equipment can still be used during a relatively short summer season. However, the incentive is high in this zone to develop ice-tolerant drilling equipment that could operate during an extended drilling season. The *third* zone comprises the northern Chukchi Sea and the Beaufort Sea shelf north of Alaska, with an average open water season of less than two months. Here conventional open water drilling methods are impractical, and special ice-resistant drilling equipment is required to explore this portion of the shelf.

As map 4-2 indicates, ice conditions improve toward the east in the Canadian Beaufort Sea. The Mackenzie Bay area normally has more than two months of open water. Canadian operators have drilled there successfully for several years with ice strengthened drillships and icebreaker support. By analogy, that same technology would be applicable in the central and southern portions of the Chukchi Sea.

Map 4-3 shows the outlines of the new Lease Planning Areas and the purposed dates for the first sale in each of these areas, according to the revised five-year schedule superimposed on Map 4-2. The technology needs for these lease areas are to a large extent dictated by two environmental parameters, water depth and open water period.

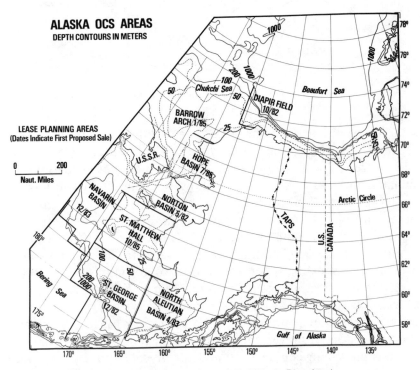

Map 4-3. Alaska Outer Continental Shelf Lease Planning Areas.

A third parameter, the severity of ice conditions in a given area, is of major significance to production operations, and will be examined later.

EXPLORATION DRILLING

In the Bering Sea, operators can use conventional equipment during the ice-free season. Some examples of semisubmersibles and ship-shaped drilling vessels were described in Chapter 3. Those would be the preferred systems on the southwestern Bering Sea Shelf in the St. George and Navarin Basins where the water is sufficiently deep for floating drilling vessels to operate. Much of the eastern shelf in the North Aleutian Basin and Norton Sound is shallower, so that bottom founded rigs could be used.

Arco used a jack-up rig to drill a stratigraphic test in Norton Sound during the summer of 1980. The rig drilled in some 65 ft of water, with the deck elevated well above the water for protection against waves and storm surges. Once a well is completed, the deck on this kind of rig is lowered into a floating position and the legs are pulled up so that the rig can be towed to another location. Conventional drilling equipment is still applicable in the Hope Basin and the central Chukchi Sea, but, increasingly, operators will be looking for ways to extend the drilling season by making their drilling systems ice tolerant or ice resistant. The first step in that direction is the use of ice-strengthened drillships. A number of drillships with ice classifications are already in the world drilling fleet. Most notable among them are the Canmar drillships used by Dome Petroleum in the Canadian Beaufort Sea. Dome has been drilling in Mackenzie Bay since 1976. A total of 12 wells have been drilled, including five yet to be completed.

Drilling operations have also been supported by a commercial ice-breaker, the *Kigoriak,* which has been used to break up ice in the vicinity of a ship, and to push ice floes and broken ice away from the ship. This has resulted in improved utilization of the drilling fleet during the summer. Nevertheless, the annual drilling season in this region has averaged less than four months. In winter, the drilling fleet, including drillships and supply vessels, must be moved to a sheltered location and frozen in for the remainder of the year. This constitutes severe underutilization of drilling equipment, and results in correspondingly high drilling costs per well.

In order to further lengthen the annual drilling season, Dome has proposed construction of a turret-moored icebreaking drillship. During the last decade, designs for such ships have been developed by other operators as well. These vessels would have an icebreaking bow, ice strengthened hull, and a special subsurface mooring system that allows the vessel to rotate in response to changes in the direction of ice movement. As a result, the ship's bow would always be headed into the direction from which the ice approaches. This orientation is optimal for icebreaking and minimizes the ice forces that must be resisted by the mooring system.

The turret-moored icebreaking drillship, if developed, should enable drilling to be extended over a substantially longer season, perhaps five to six months, in the Canadian Beaufort Sea than is currently possible with conventionally moored drillships. In addition, such a vessel may find application for winter drilling in the southern Chukchi Sea and in the northern Bering Sea.

It is difficult to make quantitative predictions as to how well such icebreaking drillships will perform in various ice conditions. But there will be limitations: One is that drilling from floating ships in moving ice or open water is likely to require water deeper than 60 ft. The polar pack ice is likely to constitute another limitation: The feasibility of drilling from floating ships in concentrated pack ice with multi-year floes remains questionable. Since the extent and movements of the polar pack ice vary seasonally from year to year, this limitation is not well defined. But for purposes of this analysis, it may be assumed that floating drilling systems, including icebreaking turret-moored drillships, may not be viable in Arctic ocean areas with less than about two months of open water. That would include the northern Chukchi Sea and most of the Alaskan portion of the Beaufort Sea.

In sum, there are two zones on the Alaskan shelf where the conventional approach to offshore drilling is not applicable: (1) shallow areas with less than 60 ft water depth along the northern Chukchi and Beaufort Sea coasts; and (2) the region of polar pack ice in the Alaskan Beaufort Sea and the Northern Chukchi Sea. A proven drilling method is available for the first zone, but drilling equipment for the second zone is still under development. The specialized Arctic drilling methods available for the first zone are man-made gravel islands, and for the second zone, conical gravity structures.

Several operators have utilized man-made islands for exploration drilling in shallow Arctic waters. This technology was developed in the Canadian Beaufort Sea, where 18 islands have been completed to date, 16 of them by Exxon's Canadian affiliate, Esso Resources Canada. Islands have been constructed both in the summer (by dredging or barging fill material) and in the winter (by trucking gravel over the ice).

The record water depth (until 1981) for a man-made island for drilling was held by the island of Issungnak in 63 ft of water in Mackenzie Bay. The island was constructed of dredged sand during three consecutive summer seasons. It features a wide sacrificial beach that acts as a buffer zone for wave erosion during the summer. The steeper slopes above this sacrificial beach are protected by sand bags. The total island volume is nearly five million cubic meters. Construction cost was about $60 million dollars. The first well drilled from the island discovered oil and gas. A second well has been drilled from this same island to help delineate the reservoir.

Drilling islands have also been used by Alaskan operators. A total of seven islands have been built, most of them by a winter construction method, that will be described briefly.

The first step is construction of an ice road. After the ice has grown to about two feet thick in early winter, lightweight vehicles are used to drill holes through the ice and lift water to the surface with an auger pump. The water spreads out and freezes, and the process is repeated on a daily basis, thickening the ice by several inches per day. The ice road may be about 400 ft wide. The extra width serves two purposes: to provide a buffer zone for snowdrifts during storms, and to allow gravel hauling and snow removal to be conducted simultaneously after a storm. Flooding may be continued for several weeks, until the ice thickness reaches the desired value, typically about seven feet. Once the road is completed, the sea ice cover is removed at the construction site. Trenching machines are used to cut the ice into blocks that can be lifted out by a backhoe and loaded onto trucks for disposal away from the island site. Then gravel is dumped into the excavated area.

Exxon built a drilling island at Beechey Point in 18 to 20 ft water depth, a few miles northeast of Prudhoe Bay. After the initial gravel pad was built upon the sea floor, additional gravel was used to enlarge the island base. At the fringe, the ice sheet was cut into blocks and lifted out of the water to make room for the gravel. All the heavy machinery operated on the gravel pad, not on the floating ice sheet, which made it a very safe operation, with minimum risk of heavy equipment breaking through the ice. The island was completed in early April 1981 after only 38 days of construction. During that time, 350,000 cubic yards of gravel were transported a distance of 12 miles from a gravel pit onshore. The island's working platform was about 14 ft high. Additional gravel was stockpiled on the island for use during the summer to fill sandbags to be placed on the slopes to prevent wave erosion. A drilling rig was to be barged to this site at the end of one summer to drill a well in the following winter. Beechey Point is in federal waters, so that before a construction permit could be obtained from the U.S. Geological Survey, the island design had to be verified by a Certified Verification Agent, pursuant to provisions in the 1981 Arctic Outer Continental Shelf Orders.

Another drilling island lies just south of the Beechey Point in about 10 ft of water, where Exxon has been drilling a well in an area known as Duck Island. During the drilling operation an ice monitoring and defense system was maintained to provide warnings in case of unusual ice movements or ice pressures. A building on top of the protective berm at the island edge served as the control center for this monitoring system. It contains instrumentation and computing facilities to analyze data from a number of sensors located on the ice around the island. Automatic alarms are sounded when unusual ice activity is detected. A trained technician was stationed in the building to maintain the equipment and to verify any alarms if they occur. Alarm levels for ice pressure were set well below the value used for island design. These alarm levels have never been reached in Exxon's drilling operations off the North Slope of Alaska.

The island construction method that has been described can be used in water deeper than 20 ft so long as safe travel over the ice is feasible by the end of winter, typically to about 40 ft of water in the Alaskan Beaufort Sea. Beyond the 40 ft water depth contour, the ice surface is often too rough and unstable to allow a sustained, large-scale gravel hauling operation. Thus, island construction by dredging during the summer would probably be more attractive in the deeper waters. Most of the Canadian islands have been built by this method. However, dredging in the Alaskan Beaufort Sea may be hampered by the presence of drift ice during most or all of the summer. To improve construction efficiency under these conditions, there is a need for ice-resistant dredging equipment and for improved methods of retaining island fill during construction to reduce both fill volume and construction time.

Improved island-building techniques are being used in offshore Canada, where Gulf Canada has initiated construction of a drilling island in 75 ft of water by using a large hopper dredge. The dredge can operate in a shuttle mode, transporting gravel or sand from a borrow pit in protected waters to an exposed construction site, dumping 10,000 cubic meters of fill material at a time. This avoids the use of a floating dredge pipeline or transport by conventional barges, both of which are subject to interruptions by the presence of drift ice.

Gulf Canada has been building an island at the Tarsiut location in 75 ft of water. Once the island base has been constructed to within 20 ft of the water surface, four large concrete caissons will be set down on the berm to form a steep-sided enclosure for the upper portion of the island. A relatively small amount of additional fill material will then be pumped into the enclosure to complete the island. The caisson-retained island concept minimizes wave erosion during construction and reduces fill volumes significantly compared to islands constructed with shallow slopes and sacrificial beach, such as the Issungnak Island described earlier. Several alternative caisson designs, featuring both steel and concrete construction, have been developed by the industry.

As the water depth increases, the construction of gravel islands becomes increasingly difficult and costly and other types of drilling platforms may become more attractive. Exxon and other oil companies have been conducting research and development work on alternative drilling methods that would be applicable in deeper Arctic waters. Among these are mobile conical gravity structures that are designed to break the ice by bending rather than crushing. This results in significantly reduced loads. Both concrete and steel structures have been proposed. An example is Esso Resources Canada's preliminary design for a conical concrete structure for water depths up to 135 ft. The structure would consist of a large, circular hull, a cone section with a 45° cone angle, and a multistory deck section. The hull is designed for impact by deep-keeled ice features and serves two main functions: (1) to provide resistance against sliding and overturning when the structure rests on bottom; and (2) to provide buoyancy when deballasted so that the structure can be towed while floating on its hull in a stable configuration and with minimum draft. This particular structure was designed for operating in the depth range from 70 to 135 ft. It has a hull diameter of 450 ft. To extend the range of applicability to deeper water, the cone structure could conceivably be set on top of a dredged subsea berm. Alternatively, several structures of different size could be constructed for use in different water depth ranges.

Cone structures must be designed to resist large multiyear pressure ridges that are embedded in the drifting pack ice. Model studies have been conducted to determine the forces that may be developed when cone structures and multiyear pressure ridges interact. For example, Exxon has conducted model tests with joint-industry funding in Esso Resources Canada's outdoor test basin in Calgary, Alberta. The model cone had a 30° slope and was approximately 1/10 scale. The model tests simulated interactions with partially consolidated ice rubble, and with fully consolidated pressure ridges up to 4 ft thick (40 ft full-scale). The ice forces measured during these experiments can be scaled up to full-scale field conditions, and the results will form the basis for improved cone structure designs for the Alaskan Beaufort Sea.

From a technical standpoint, it is anticipated that with the further development of conical drilling structures, drilling capability in the 100 to 200 ft water depth range can be attained within the next seven to ten years. This technology would be applicable mainly in the Alaskan Beaufort Sea and in the northern Chukchi Sea, beyond the limits of gravel islands and floating drilling systems. However, the large anticipated cost of these structures and their limited applicability to a relatively narrow water depth range on the Arctic Ocean shelf will require the acquisition of leases prior to their final construction. Lease terms, therefore, should provide for a lead time of several years before the onset of exploration drilling.

PRODUCTION PLATFORMS

In contrast to exploration drilling systems, production platforms must remain on location year-round and must be designed to withstand extreme environmental conditions likely to be encountered during the structure's lifetime. Determining the appropriate design criteria, therefore, is an important part of the engineering effort that goes into the selection of a platform concept and its final design. The petroleum industry has undertaken extensive studies to determine the optimal operating and design conditions for the various Alaskan OCS areas. They have included wave measurements with instrumented buoys, earthquake monitoring with seismometers placed on the sea floor, and sea ice surveys using aerial photography and other remote sensing equipment, in addition to direct observations and measurements on the surface. This information is being used for screening studies and preliminary design work to identify applicable platform types on a regional basis.

Once a discovery is made, the design information must be supplemented by site-specific data, including data on local soil conditions. Only then can a detailed final platform design be developed. The ultimate design may be somewhat different from the general platform types that will be described. In any case, the design studies carried out to-date have identified feasible and practical platform concepts for each of the various sedimentary basins in the Alaskan OCS, most of them being direct extensions of existing technology.

Upper Cook Inlet near Anchorage Alaska is a sea ice environment where offshore platforms have been in operation since the early 1960s. Fourteen platforms were built there between 1964 and 1968. Some unique designs, like the monopod structure, were developed to cope with ice floes up to 3-1/2 ft thick, moving back and forth with swift tidal currents. All of the Cook Inlet structures are characterized by large caisson-like legs and an elaborate piling system. To minimize exposure to the sea ice, the wells are drilled through the legs, eliminating external well conductors, and there are no braces between the legs in the vicinity of the water level. Pile-founded structures like those in Cook Inlet may find application in other sub-Arctic sea ice areas with relatively shallow water, for instance, the North Aleutian Basin or Norton Sound.

Farther to the west, in the St. George and Navarin Basins, the deeper water and the remoteness of the area will tend to favor gravity-type structures, which can be installed with a minimum of on-site construction and with most or all of the deck facilities already in place. Gravity structures were first used in the North Sea. A conventional three-legged concrete gravity structure, for example, can support large deck loads and, due to their large mass, can also resist large lateral loads exerted by waves or sea ice. Their principal limitation is that firm foundation soils are required to resist (1) the large overturning moment developed by sheet ice crushing against the legs, and (2) the large base shear forces induced by earthquakes. Given adequate soil conditions, such as firm sand or stiff clay, this type of structure might be designed for water depths from 300 to 500 ft in the St. George area.

Modified gravity tower concepts may be used to accommodate soft foundation soils. A monotower structure can be designed to minimize ice loads, by supporting the deck on a single tower, equipped with an optional ice breaking cone section, and mitigate earthquake forces, by reducing the mass of the entire structure. Based on preliminary design studies, structures of this type appear feasible for the St. George and Navarin Basins in the water depth range from 300 to 650 ft.

In the Arctic, gravel islands are the most generally applicable production platform concept for shallow water. Islands are attractive because of simplicity of design and construction, and their virtually unlimited load-carrying capacity. Up to 1982, the industry had built only temporary islands for exploration drilling. However, they were designed to resist environmental forces year-round, and a number of them have been exposed to very significant ice movement events. Typically, islands in more than 20-ft water depths in the Canadian Beaufort Sea become surrounded by extensive rubble piles during the course of the winter season. But the drilling islands were not affected by the ice-movement and pile-up events, and drilling operations were not interrupted. Production islands will have to be designed for more extreme ice events than the temporary drilling islands. However, this can be easily accomplished by increasing their size and freeboard.

As in the case of exploration islands, no definite water depth limit can be given for production islands. The duration of the construction season will play a significant role in determining the economic water depth limit for island concepts. In Mackenzie Bay, with about two months of open water, islands are being considered for production and terminal operations in water depths up to 200 ft. Off the North Slope of Alaska, the open-water season is significantly shorter than in Mackenzie Bay, and the economic limit of island construction is likely to be in the 60 to 100 ft water depth range. Beyond this limit, cone gravity structures are a prime candidate for production platforms in water depths up to perhaps 200 ft. It is expected that these platform types would develop from the mobile cone structures that may be used for exploration drilling in the Beaufort and Chukchi Seas. Conical production platforms may also have application in the Hope and Norton Basins.

Large caisson islands, made of concrete or steel, are another alternative for Arctic production platforms. A concrete island would look similar to the base of a North Sea gravity structure. The diameter might be on the order of 500 ft. The outer concrete walls would have to be several feet thick to resist local ice pressure developed during crushing failure of multiyear ice. Resistance against lateral sliding would be increased by filling all or most of the structure with pumped sand. Exxon has been developing a preliminary design for a structure of this type for 60-ft water depths in the Beaufort Sea. Structures for deeper water, 150 ft or more, also appear feasible.

CONCLUSION

An assessment of Arctic drilling and production technology for sea ice areas on the Alaskan OCS indicates that existing gravel island technology can be used for year-round exploration drilling in the Alaskan Beaufort Sea out to at least 40-ft and probably 60-ft water depths. Mobile conical gravity structures are being developed for exploration drilling in water depths beyond the economic limit of gravel islands in the Beaufort Sea and in the northern Chukchi Sea. Conventional offshore drilling techniques are suitable during the open-water season in the Bering Sea and the southern Chukchi Sea. Icebreaking drillships may be used to extend the drilling season in these areas.

If discoveries were made in any of these areas, ice resistance platforms would be required for development drilling and production operations. Man-made production islands would be applicable in shallow water of the Beaufort, Chukchi, and perhaps the Northern Bering Sea.

Cone-shaped production platforms or other types of gravity platforms, such as concrete islands, are likely candidates in the same areas in deeper water, out to 150 to 200 ft. Cook Inlet type steel structures with pile-foundations could be used in the North Aleutian area and perhaps also in Norton Sound. Finally, various adaptations of gravity tower concepts, proven in the North Sea, would be applicable on the deeper portions of the Bering Sea shelf, in the St. George and Navarin basins.

Feasible platform types have been identified for all the sedimentary basins on the Alaskan OCS scheduled for leasing in the 1981 five-year plan. The oil industry can begin to design platforms for site-specific environmental conditions and for specific operational requirements as soon as a discovery is made. The industry has spent much time, money, and effort on engineering research and on environmental studies to develop operational capabilities to explore, develop, and produce in all Arctic areas. These efforts will continue in the future to insure that operational capability will be available in a time frame that is consistent with the proposed OCS leasing schedule.

Chapter 5
Pipelines for Offshore Gas and Oil

Don E. Lambert

The future of offshore pipelines will be determined by four factors:
1) the discovery of oil and gas reserves large enough to justify costly
subsea pipe lines — some of which will be among the most expensive
projects ever undertaken by private enterprise; 2) the generation of
enough capital within a realistic time frame to meet the financial requirements of some of the projects that are envisioned; 3) the development of new technology and services that will permit laying, recovery,
and repair of pipe lines in water depths to 6,500 ft or more; 4) political stability among those nations planning some of the huge projects that may span two continents.

Bechtel, Inc. has reported that some 25 percent of the world's remaining oil reserves are offshore. Although the unit cost for offshore
development may go as high as 20 times greater than for onshore development, world prices in the early 1980s have made it more profit-
able to develop production from the seabed. As onshore supplies are
depleted, attention will be increasingly focused upon offshore resources. Recent projections have shown a rise from 18.5 percent in
1980 to about 27 percent by the year 2000 in offshore oil's contribution to total world oil production. Bechtel also reports it recently
completed a marine survey and mapped the route for a 120-mile gas
pipe line that would extend across the western Mediterranean from
Algeria to Spain through waters exceeding 6,500 feet in depth. This
project will be discussed in detail later.

Indicative of the rise of offshore gas and oil development with important consequences for the pipe laying industry after a two-year lull
was an announcement by ETPM of France, one of the world's largest
offshore construction firms, that the ETPM Group had achieved in

1980 a turnover of $291 million and would probably have a turnover in excess of $350 million in 1981. On 12 May 1981 the company more than doubled its working capital from $9 million to $19.4 million.

Some of the more important contracts awarded since February 1981 included the huge lay vessel ETPM 1601, flagship of the ETPM fleet, which has been laying pipelines up to 48 inches in diameter in Mexico's Bay of Campeche. In 1982, the ETPM 1601 went to Australia to lay a 36-inch gas pipe line 84 miles (135 km) on the Northwest Shelf for the Woodside Company. ETPM will also design, fabricate, and install platforms and an oil terminal in India's offshore Ratnagiri oil field. In the Persian Gulf, in joint venture with a state-owned company, ETPM will install a water injection complex in the Zakum oil field off the coast of Abu Dhabi. In Cameroon, ETPM will construct and install 10 platforms and several flow lines in the Cameroon Mokoko-Abana offshore field. ETPM has also signed several contracts in Nigeria with Gulf Oil and Texaco for the Funiwa and Okubi fields, and with NNPC, the national petroleum company, for the installation of an oil terminal at Escravios-Warri. And ETPM has signed a contract with Gulf Oil for development of the Takula field in Angola.

This was the first time since its creation in 1965 that ETPM had signed and booked such an amount of orders and contracts. Similar reports could be made for Brown and Root, Bechtel, Fluor, Saipem, Snamprogetti, and other major engineering/construction firms.

The optimism of the pipeline industry about 1981 and 1982 was indicated in January 1981 when *Pipe Line Industry* projected a 362-mile increase in worldwide offshore pipelaying in the next twelve months to 2,653 miles – up nearly 16 percent over 1980.

Thus, the evidence is strong that the four factors – oil and gas reserves, capital generation, new technology and political stability – have been working in harmony. Whether this will be true for the huge projects that lie ahead remains to be seen. Assuming that the factors will remain favorable, it will be useful to examine the several areas of major offshore gas and oil development to compare their potential for the pipeline industry.

UNITED STATES

In January 1981, *Pipe Line Industry* estimated 985 miles of pipelines would be laid off U.S. coasts that year. Companies that replied to the "Construction Scoreboard" of the journal reported 785 miles were under way or scheduled for construction in 1981. Other projects were to be completed between 1 June and 31 December. Thus, the January forecast appeared to be on target. As usual, nearly all of the pipeline mileage was off the coasts of Texas and Louisiana. The activity off California and Alaska mostly involved gathering line construction. Although the Transcontinental Gas Pipe Line Corporation announced a proposal to lay a gas line from the Baltimore Canyon off New Jersey and Delaware to East Coast onshore facilities, construction has not started on the project and may never begin. The Tennessee Gas Pipe Line Company and others have discovered gas in the area, but initial production indicates that the reserves are not significant enough to justify a pipeline in the near future.

By the summer of 1981, companies had announced plans to lay more than 400 miles of U.S. offshore pipelines in 1982. One of 1982's projects was the largest ever in Texas waters. State government authorities have been considering two competing proposals: 250 miles of 24-inch pipe by Corpus Christi Oil and Gas Company, and 275 miles of 14-inch pipe by Seagull Pipeline Corporation.

The laying of pipelines in offshore waters, of course, depends upon the discovery of economically viable oil and gas reserves. In turn, the discovery and production of new reserves ultimately depends on the acreage made available for wildcatting. The erratic scheduling of the government's offshore oil and gas lease auctions from 1975 to 1980 has delayed exploration and production. Under the present schedule for the next five years, the best that can be hoped for is to maintain the current exploration, pipeline construction, and production levels.

The five-year schedule inherited from the Carter Administration called for 36 lease sales. The revised schedule announced jointly by Interior Secretary James Watt and Energy Secretary James Edwards in 1981 called for 42 lease sales during the period, offered more acreage in each sale, and expected to open up areas off Alaska's coast sooner. With these incentives, there was a fair chance that significant new reserves would be found, requiring the construction of more offshore pipelines.

CANADA

In Canada huge gas and oil reserves have been found in two of the world's most hostile environments: the 1,000-by-2,000 mile Hibernia area off the coasts of Newfoundland and Labrador, described by some sources as "similar to the North Sea, but with icebergs," and in the Canadian Arctic Islands, with their own environmental challenge.

There has been considerable study of ways to produce and transport the Hibernia reserves, for everything depends on the industry's ability to protect subsea installations and pipelines from icebergs. In the 1979 iceberg seas, 400 bergs floated through the Hibernia area. During the 1980 season, no bergs passed through. But there were 1,200 bergs in the 1978 season, and a record number of 1,400 bergs passed through the area in 1974. The bergs can weigh from eight to twelve million tons and can create scours in the seabed measuring from 100 to 150 ft in width. The deepest scours to date are about 6 ft in the Hibernia area and 15 ft in the Avalon area.

A large pipeline construction area would be opened up for the Hibernian reserves if the decision were to use this transportation mode. Excavation of a glory hole to a 50-ft depth using clamshell dredging would be technically feasible. However, trenching in bedrock is not presently feasible and not likely in the foreseeable future. A proposed northern pipeline route, which has the problem of trenching through bedrock, does not appear feasible, but a southern route cannot be ruled out, although a little longer than the northern route, because it does not have the problem of trenching through bedrock. The southern route would need to trench to depths of 12 to 27 ft in surficial sediments, which does not appear to be a serious obstacle. Although the immediate use of pipelines may not be economic, future discoveries of resources might well change the financial considerations in favor of pipelines.

In Canada's Arctic Islands, Polar Gas has selected the pipeline mode as the best means of transportation of large volumes of natural gas from the frontier regions to southern markets. Two marine crossings will be necessary at the north and south ends of Victoria Island. The marine and climatic conditions are quite different at each crossing. The simpler crossing, at Dolphin and Union Strait, can be accomplished with modified laybarge techniques. Dolphin and Union Strait is relatively narrow — only 19 miles across and about 400 ft deep. Although winter ice averages seven ft in thickness, the summer usually has more than two months of open water. Tunnels will protect the pipe line at both shore approaches from potential ice scour.

The northern crossing, at M'Clure Strait, is not nearly so simple. M'Clure is more than 75 miles wide, and more than 1,600 ft deep. During winter, ice can range up to 40 ft thick. Frequently, the ice cover persists right through the summer. Despite these surface conditions, which also include February temperatures as low as 35 degress below zero, bathymetric studies indicate that the seabed is quite adequate for supporting a subsea pipe line.

After several years of intensive study, it has been determined that a marine pipeline can be laid across M'Clure Strait with the "Ice Hole Bottom Pull" method developed by Polar Gas. Long strings of pipe are pulled into place on the seabed from holes cut in the ice surface.

Thus, the pipelining of natural gas from the High Arctic is now economically viable in light of proved reserves — more than 16 trillion cubic feet — and the upward trend in gas prices. Polar gas has also been certain that such projects are technically feasible. This certainly has come from the success of an April 1978 project when the world's first subsea production gas well was connected to production facilities onshore. A 3,600-ft-flowline bundle was connected to the wellhead by a diverless subsea flowline connector.

Development of wells in the Sverdrup Basin of the Arctic Islands will require an extensive gas gathering network that will connect wells up to 12 miles offshore in water up to 1,200 ft deep. In eastern Canada's gas-rich Sable Island area, pipeline plans have been discussed. But until enough gas reserves are found, a holding pattern will continue. This will be true in the wildcatting areas all along the continental shelves of Labrador, Newfoundland, and Nova Scotia.

MEXICO

The major pipelining area of Mexico has been a beehive of activity. During the 1980s high priority will be given to gas pipelines and the compressor stations needed to move offshore gas from the Campeche Sound area to onshore facilities. The country's state-owned oil and gas entity, Pemex, reported that in 1981 that it was flaring more than 550 million cubic feet of gas per day in Campeche Sound and other producing areas. As a result, Mexico will continue to be an active pipelining country for several years.

SOUTH AMERICA

South America's quest for self-sufficiency in oil and gas has created an unprecedented drilling boom, particularly in Argentina and Brazil. Drilling activity is at an all-time high in both countries, with the offshore areas playing a major role. During the rest of this decade, offshore pipelining for these states as well as for Chile, Bolivia, Columbia, Peru, Uruguay, and Ecuador will be an important activity.

Brazil's Campos Basin is South America's most active offshore oil and gas producing area. In fact, the longest offshore oil and gas pipelines in South America were under construction in 1981 to move the production to shore. The $438 million pipe line plan was designed to carry up to 440,000 barrels of crude and 3.5 billion cubic feet of gas per day from permanent production platforms to terminals and a refinery near Rio de Janeiro. J. Ray McDermott won the $86 million contract to lay the 532-km (330-mile) pipeline system, while another U.S. firm, Morrison Knudsen, received the contract for concrete coating of the pipe. The gas line and the oil line were to be completed before 1983.

THE NORTH SEA

In the North Sea a massive offshore pipeline construction program has been planned to link several gas fields, now noncommercial, with onshore markets. With new discoveries continuing and no less than three gathering systems in prospect, the North Sea's ability to supply more gas to European mainland markets is assured. Great Britain, Norway, and Denmark have 1,300 miles of gas lines in the planning stage. Since construction will overlap to some degree, there will be a concentrated demand for pipelaying capacity. It would be more efficient for the three countries to join together in one huge project to serve their needs and those of mainland Europe, but it appears that there is little hope that this will happen. Great Britain and Norway were expected to start construction on separate projects in 1983.

Italy's Saipem has plans to move its highly sophisticated lay barge *Castoro Sei* to the North Sea, thereby joining the big semisubmersibles *Viking Piper* and *Semac 1,* and becoming part of the world's largest construction fleet for what is likely to be the biggest offshore pipelaying undertaking of the 1980s.

Great Britain's £2.74 billion ($5 billion) gathering system has both government and industry support. It apparently needs only to solve minor organizational problems before starting construction in 1983. It will be a 600-mile system originating at the Statfjord field in the northern North Sea and the Fulmar field in the south. The north and south legs will join at a platform in the T block, close to the Norwegian line, and continue on to the expanding St. Fergus, Scotland terminal. The north leg will be 208 miles of 36-inch pipe, the south leg will be 148 miles of 20-inch pipe, and the line from the T block to the St. Fergus terminal will be 136 miles of 36-inch pipe. The north leg will serve 11 fields, not yet in production, and the south leg will serve 5 fields, through about 100 miles of laterals. It will be a high pressure system, with an input pressure of 2,500 psig and an outlet pressure of 1,600 psig to avoid the need for intermediate compression. Without intermediate compression, the system will be capable of handling a large volume of natural gas liquids.

The Norwegian Ministry of Petroleum and Energy reported that the Norwegian pipe line system will be landed in Norway and in operation by the target date of 1985–86.

A key element in the project is the Statfjord field where gas has been recycled. This practice can continue only at the risk of damaging the producing formation and should be discontinued by 1985. Considering the lead time involved in designing, building, and bringing a pipeline into operation, that is a rather short interval if construction does not start until 1983.

Of the companies operating the Norwegian portion of the Statfjord field, 84 percent have proposed a $3.4 billion, 30-inch pipe gathering system, about 550 miles in length. The system will consist of a pipeline from Statfjord to Karsto on the mainland, another from Karsto to the Ekofisk field with an intermediate compressor platform;

and a third from the Heimdal field to the compressor platform. Liquids will be removed from the gas at Karsto. The gas will move from Ekofisk through the existing 36-inch pipe line to Emden, West Germany. The system will involve two crossings of the 1,000-ft to 1,200-ft deep Norwegian trench, once regarded as a virtually impassable barrier to pipelines. Since the *Castoro Sei* has laid pipelines in 2,000-ft water depths in crossing the Sicilian channel, crossing the Norwegian trench should not pose a major problem.

Continental European interests want the Norwegian gas so badly that they are willing to underwrite the cost of a pipeline that would by-pass Ekofisk and go direct to Emden. A guiding element in Norway's decision has been its policy of developing its North Sea resources so that future as well as present generations will benefit from them.

The system proposed by the Statfjord operators will handle initially about 800 million cubic feet of gas per day with 400 million cubic feet per day originating at Statfjord, 300 from Heimdal, and 100 from the 34/10 block. The addition of other fields in the future could raise the throughput to as much as 1.5 million cubic feet per day. This proposal would skip Sleipner, one of Norway's largest gas fields.

The third prospective North Sea gas gathering system would be in the Danish sector. It would include a 133-mile main line from the Tyra, West Tyra, Roar, Gorm, Skjold, and Dan fields, which would deliver the gas to Esbjerg on the mainland. The system would include the 133-mile main line from the Tyra field to Esbjerg and 38 miles of 10-inch pipe gathering lines.

The gas gathering systems by reasons of their size, no matter what plan is accepted, dominate the North Sea pipeline construction picture, but still are only part of it. Other projects in the immediate future are a 57-mile, 24-inch crude oil pipeline from the Magnus to the Ninian field; a 44-mile, 24-inch pipeline from the West Sole field to Easington; a 30-mile, 36-inch pipeline from the Rough field to Easington — all in the British sector; and two in the Dutch sector — one of 110 miles from the F quadrant and one of 50 miles from the P quadrant.

The Magnus field and the West Sole field pipe lines will be laid by the *Castoro Sei* after it completes an overhaul at Spezia, Italy.

AFRICA

Most of the current pipeline activity in Africa involves the laying of flow lines and some trunk lines to shore. A dramatic milestone in offshore pipeline technology was the construction of three parallel 20-inch gas lines 100 miles across the Mediterranean from Cap Bon, Tunisia to Sicily, then across the Messina Strait to the Italian mainland. It led the way for the planning of several ultra-deepwater pipelines that are in various stages of development throughout the world. In fact, another project has been under study that will even overshadow the history-making Algeria-Tunisia-Sicily-Italy gas system. Nigeria has been studying the economic and technical feasibility of laying a 36-inch or larger gas pipe line more than 2,500 miles through Niger and Algeria, then through smaller diameter lines, across the Mediterranean Sea to West Europe markets.

One proposal is to parallel the existing transmediterranean pipeline with extensions from Italy north into West Europe. The other proposal, which would lead to one of the most ambitious undertakings in the history of pipelining, would involve building the Nigeria pipeline to Arzew, Algeria, then across the Mediterranean in 6,500-ft water depths to Almeria, Spain, where it would extend northward into France and other countries of western Europe.

The cost of such a project, estimated at more than $10 billion, would appear to be far out of reach of most financial sources. However, considering that Nigeria has 50 trillion cubic feet of natural gas reserves worth $250 billion dollars, if priced at $5.00 per thousand cubic feet, the cost doesn't seem quite so prohibitive. Nigeria also has been studying a $15 billion Liquid Natural Gas (LNG) complex to serve energy-hungry markets with tankers. But there is a good possibility that the pipeline will be built instead.

Returning to more immediate projects in Africa, Italy's Snamprogetti has been awarded a major contract for the development of oil reserves offshore Egypt. The project consists of a number of offshore platforms interconnected by flow lines, submarine oil and gas pipe lines, and a water reinjection line. The development will be for the Ras Budran oil field, some three miles offshore on the eastern side of the Gulf of Suez, in 120 ft of water.

THE PERSIAN GULF

Offshore pipelining never stops in the Persian Gulf, sometimes called the Arabian Gulf or the Gulf. One of the more interesting projects in this area has been at Abu Dhabi where the Zakum Development Company has been laying 466 miles of crude oil pipelines to develop the Upper Zakum offshore field. The Upper Zakum project is being coordinated with construction of a Lower Zakum gas gathering system. Eventually this project would involve about 138 miles of 6 to 48-inch pipe. Thus, a crude oil pipe line system was being constructed on top of a gas pipeline system, and the result will be a spaghetti-like network of more than 600 miles of offshore gathering and flow lines.

SOUTHERN ASIA

There are two active areas of offshore gas and oil recovery in Southern Asia, India and Thailand. India's Oil and Natural Gas Commission has been considering two different routes to carry natural gas from the South Bassein field to coastal consuming areas. One route calls for a 62-mile offshore pipeline from South Bassein to Nawapour. The second route calls for a 143-mile, 36-inch pipeline to be laid offshore from South Bassein to Ubhrat. Although studies indicate that the long distance offshore project would cost less and could be built in only one season, the route to Nawapour solves political problems. The government has promised that the states of Gujarat and Mahashtra, along the Nawapour route, would have equal shares in the offshore gas.

Construction of the first phase of an extensive gas collection, transmission, and treatment project was underway in 1981 in the Gulf of Thailand. Fluor Ocean Services was engineering the job and Brown and Root was laying the offshore lines. The project was divided into two phases, with the first phase involving construction of a 369-mile natural gas pipeline from Union Oil's production platform in the Gulf of Thailand to an onshore terminal at Juksamet in Rayong province. In phase 2, a 105-mile system will connect Texas Pacific's offshore platform with Union's platform. The offshore sections of pipe will be 34 inches in diameter with 0.625-inch wall thickness.

WESTERN PACIFIC

In the Western Pacific, Australia is by far the most active area for pipelines. Development of the country's largest natural resource project, the Northwest Shelf, is in progress. As mentioned earlier, France's ETPM 1601 lay vessel will lay the line that will carry natural gas from the Northwest Shelf fields to shore near Dampier. The 81-mile submarine pipe line will be 36 inches in diameter.

In other Western Pacific areas, several hundred miles of offshore gathering line and trunklines are in various stages of development in New Zealand, Malaysia, Indonesia, and Japan.

FUTURE PIPELINE ACTIVITY

Pipe Line Industry forecast that nearly 10,000 miles of offshore trunk and gathering lines would be laid from 1981 through 1985, substantially more than the 8,460 miles reported during the 1976–1980 five-year period. Playing a key role in this hectic scramble to link all economically viable offshore reserves with world markets, the North Sea again will set the pace, with about 2,200 miles of trunk lines and 1,500 miles of gathering systems. Other active 1981–1985 areas for pipelines will include the Middle East and Africa, with about 2,000 miles of pipe; Southeast Asia and Western Pacific, with about 1,800 miles; the Gulf of Mexico, with about 1,700 miles; and South America, with about 850 miles.

Capital outlays for offshore pipelines and related facilities during the next five years are expected to exceed $25 billion. This large increase in spending, compared with $12 billion during the previous five years, is attributed to inflation and to expensive construction in some of the world's most hostile environments, such as Arctic Islands, the Norwegian trench, and the 6,500-ft water depths for the SEGAMO trans-Mediterranean project.

In July 1977, an editorial in *Pipe Line Industry* suggested that the next 15 years would see the greatest offshore construction boom in history if governments permitted it. A British survey had forecast 3,800–4,000 miles of offshore pipe lines would be laid throughout the world during 1977–1983, and that most of the construction, between 2,450 and 2,900 miles, would be expected during the 1979–1983 period.

Moreover, the 1977 editorial noted that the Bechtel Corp. predicted that the future of offshore pipelining, at least for the next 10 years, would be very good, something on the order of 40,000 miles, which would average out at 4,000 miles per year, considerably higher than any other forecast.

Sante Fe International also had prepared an area-by-area projection for 1977 and 1978, and, in the Gulf of Mexico, Santa Fe estimated that about 676 miles of pipelines per year would be installed; in the Middle East, about 400 miles per year; and in other areas, about 460 miles in 1977 and 725 in 1978. The North Sea was projected to be an area of "pause" during 1977 and 1978, with construction totaling between 350 and 375 miles annually. The company's long range forecast predicted a significant increase in construction mileage during 1979 and 1980.

Pipe Line Industry, in its 1977 editorial, forecast capital expenditures for worldwide offshore construction to total more than $12 billion during the next five years alone, with about 8,000 miles of trunklines and 4,000 miles of gathering lines being laid during this period.

The editorial noted that there were projects that would test man's ingenuity to the fullest, both in terms of new technology and obtaining capital to finance them, including pipelines in 1,200-ft water depths from the Statfjord field area to Norway and, possibly, a 600-mile, 42-inch, $2.5 billion huge gas-gathering pipe line from the northern North Sea to West Germany, the SEGAMO gas project from Algeria to Spain, which would include a 121-mile Mediterranean Sea crossing in water depths to 6,500 ft, gas pipelines to connect Canada's Arctic islands with the mainland, the development of Australia's Northwest Shelf, and many others.

Finally, the 1977 editorial stated that hundreds of millions of dollars were being spent to develop methods and equipment for construction, maintenance and repair of pipelines in 1,000-ft plus water depths and under severe Arctic conditions, and that industry was doing its part to make huge offshore gas and oil reserves available to energy-deficient nations.

Nearly all of the major projects in hostile environments reported in that 1977 editorial to be under study have taken shape, and the destiny of nearly all of these projects is still under the control of the national governments, whether in the North Sea, the Mediterranean, Australia's Northwest Shelf, or Canada's Arctic Islands.

TECHNOLOGICAL DEVELOPMENT

Only in 1974 did ultra-deepwater technology for pipe lines start to emerge on a large scale, with the North Sea as the testing ground. First came the expensive superbarges and self-propelled vessels in different configurations that were needed to lay the pipe in water depths below 500 ft, such as France's $40 million self-propelled pipelay/derrick ship *ETPM 1601*. Since 1974 the *ETPM 1601* has worked in the Gulf of Mexico, in Argentina's Strait of Magellan, and is scheduled to lay pipe on Australia's Northwest Shelf.

After the *ETPM 1601* came the huge $65 million semisubmersible *Viking Piper,* capable of laying 44-inch pipe lines in 1,200 ft of water — it was put to work in the North Sea in 1975.

The following years of 1976 and 1977 were key years for deep-water pipelaying capability. Among the new barges and vessels were the self-propelled reel vessel *Apache,* capable of laying 24-inch pipe from a huge reel in 3,000 ft of water; the *Semac 1,* a twin-hull semi-submersible barge; Brown and Root's *Bar 347,* a conventional lay-barge, capable of laying 36-inch pipe in 1,100 ft of water. *Bar 347* is 660 ft long, longer than two football fields, 140 ft wide, and 50 ft deep. Other units introduced during this two-year period were the *D.L.B. 1602,* sister ship to the *ETPM 1601;* and Japan's *Kuroshiro II* derrick/laybarge.

In 1978, Italy's $150 million *Castoro Sei* propulsion-assisted pipe-laying vessel was launched. Its first job was to lay three parallel 20-inch gas pipe lines across the Mediterranean Sea from Tunisia to Italy in record-setting water depths below 2,000 ft. Also in 1978, Martech International's reel barge, capable of laying pipe in 1,000-ft water depths, was put to work in the Gulf of Mexico.

New technology is being developed that once again promises to revolutionize offshore pipe laying. Some time during the next 10 years, pipelines may be welded by electron beams or the flash butt method, using the J-curve rather than current S-curve pipelay concept. France's TOTAL Group has completed preliminary plans for an in-clined lay ramp and an electron beam welding machine suitable for offshore use, possibly to lay pipe across the Mediterranean in 6,500 ft of water for the SEGAMO project that was described earlier.

Electron beam welding involves an orbital welding system with mobile electron beam guns. The guns are automatically aimed at the joint plane. Welding takes place in a vacuum. The vacuum joint is a continuous reinforced elastomer seal that is capable of accommodating large movements. The automatic alignment system has been tested with 20-inch diameter pipe, demonstrating that the system gives accurate alignment without the need to measure clearances and that structural deformation to the pipe end will not occur.

The German Group ARGE PIPE-J-pbw has developed a welding system and station to flash butt weld pipe connections after inductive preheating. The pipe joints are rigidly clamped close to the ends, preheated by induction, brought together for the flashing operation, and then upset. This method permits offshore use of J-curve pipe laying. Extensive studies have shown that the J-method of pipe laying can substantially increase the water depth capability for 20-inch pipe to about 9,850 ft. For 40-inch pipe, the depth can be increased to about 3,950 ft. Test results have indicated that flash butt welding produces rapid, high quality welds.

The flash butt method offers the advantages of lower horizontal forces, which affect the lay vessel positioning; allowing the elimination of large tension machines and the lay vessel stinger. The dimensions of the welding machine are 26 x 20 ft.

Another interesting technical development took place in May 1981 when a pipeline nearly two miles long moved down a track near Wick, Scotland, into the North Sea. Kestrel Marine assembled the pipeline onshore; then it was launched, like a submarine 10,000 ft long. The pipeline, a flow line bundle with three smaller pipes inside, built for Occidental Petroleum, was floated about 100 ft beneath the water surface buoyed by the air inside. With a seagoing tug attached by cable at either end, the flow line was towed to a site in the Claymore field.

New technologies are also emerging for support equipment, ranging from remote controlled trenching and burying machines to one atmosphere welding habitats.

The technological developments for the pipeline industry to provide rapid, efficient, economic service are already at hand. All that remains is the discovery of huge deepwater oil and gas reserves, generation of enough capital to meet the large financial requirements, and the steady support of national governments in a climate of political stability. The industry has done its part. The rewards of oil and gas in the next decade will depend upon the wildcatters, the financiers, and the national governments. With their initiative and mutual assistance, a record-shattering decade of 10,000 miles of offshore pipelines will become a reality.

Chapter 6
Buoy Loading of Tankers in Offshore Oil Fields

Roland E. Bulow
Scott G. Withee

During the late 1970s, the offshore loading of crude oil tankers was carried out under conditions that seemed utterly prohibitive earlier in the decade. As the 1980s advance, experience indicates that a well-designed system of storage, mooring/loading, and offtake vessels will be able to transport oil efficiently from virtually any offshore field. As the exploration for and the exploitation of oil continues to move farther from land into the sea, more oil fields will utilize offshore loading.

In this chapter the basic characteristics of offshore loading systems will be described and the optimal use of such systems will be analyzed. To do this will require a brief history and description of offshore loading facilities currently in service; a list of conditions that would favor offshore loading over pipeline transportation; notes on the methods for evaluating components of an offshore loading system; and an examination of techniques for estimating overall performance capabilities of an offshore storage, loading, and marine transportation system.

The descriptions of facilities in the following section, necessarily brief, are intended to introduce this equipment to those unfamiliar with offshore loading systems while providing a background for the subsequent sections. There is a considerable variety in these complex facilities. More detailed descriptions can be found in the notes to this chapter as well as in offshore trade journals and in the proceedings of various annual conferences which specialize in offshore technology.

HISTORY AND DESCRIPTIONS OF FACILITIES

Buoys

Offshore loading buoys were first used in conjunction with production facilities located on land, where the shoreline was either too congested or too shallow to permit tankers to load at conventional wharves. The two buoy designs that have become the industry standards for protected areas, in water depths up to about 120 ft, are the Catenary Anchor Leg Mooring (CALM) and the Single Anchor Leg Mooring (SALM).

The CALM, shown in Figure 6-1, was first employed around 1960. It comprises a flat cylindrical buoy moored by an array of anchor chains, a submarine hose connected to a submarine pipeline, and a swivel table atop the buoy, to which are connected the floating loading hose and the mooring lines for the tankers. During tanker loading, oil flows through the submarine pipeline, the submarine hose, the buoy, and the floating hoses, to the tanker. The swivel table permits the tanker to rotate completely around the CALM if the wind shifts during loading. By 1981 more than 100 CALM units had been put into service worldwide.

The SALM, shown in Figure 6-2, was developed in the late 1960s. It consists of a vertical cylindrical buoy moored by a single chain connected to a piled base on the sea floor. The tanker loading hose is connected to a swivel at the base; the mooring hawser is connected to the buoy. As with the CALM, the tanker can rotate to any position during loading. Three SALM's were planned to be used in the Louisiana Offshore Oil Port (LOOP).

In the mid-1970s, several large offshore oil fields under development in the North Sea required high-efficiency offshore loading systems. The proven CALM and SALM buoys were not employed because severe weather conditions were expected to damage the floating hoses frequently and also make the buoys inaccessible for extended periods. In addition, the water was more than twice the depth of previous buoy installations, so that new designs were considered necessary.

The Exposed Location Single Buoy Mooring (ELSBM), in service since January 1976 in the Auk Field,[1] addressed the problem of hose

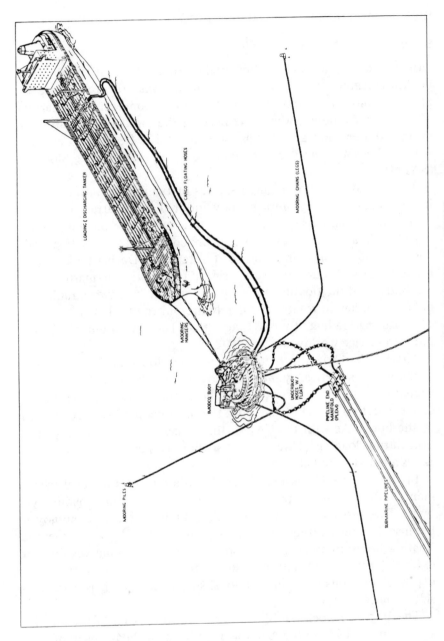

Figure 6-1. Catenary Anchor Leg Mooring (CALM).

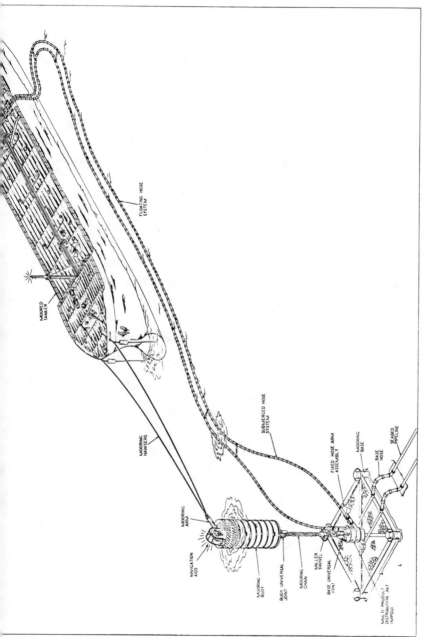

Figure 6-2. Single Anchor Leg Mooring (SALM).

damage by utilizing reels to stow the loading hose and mooring hawser when not in use. The buoy is fitted with an array of anchor chains, a pair of submarine hoses, and a helicopter deck to permit access for repair. The buoy is unmanned and located in a water depth of about 280 ft.

The Articulated Loading Platform (ALP) shown in Figure 6-3, was first used in the Beryl Field in September 1976.[2] The ALP comprises a rigid buoyant column connected to a weighted anchor base by a universal joint. A rotating head on top of the column is fitted with a hose boom, and a helicopter deck which is about 100 ft above waterline. The mooring hawser is attached to the head below the hose boom, so that if the wind shifts during loading, the head will be pulled around by the hawser and the hose boom will follow the tanker into the downwind position. Because of its buoyancy, the column tends to remain vertical and to act as a spring to keep the tanker on station. During loading the oil flows from a seabed pipeline, through the base and universal joint, up inside the column, through a swivel in the head, and through the boom and hose to the tanker. Between loadings,

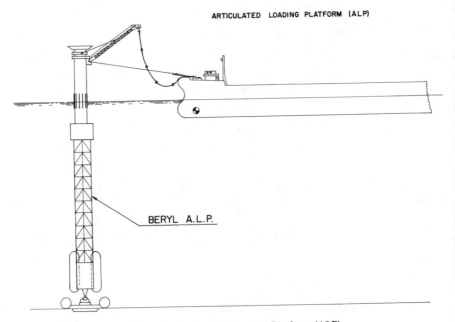

ARTICULATED LOADING PLATFORM (ALP)

BERYL A.L.P.

Figure 6-3. Articulated Loading Platform (ALP).

the hose hangs vertically from the boom tip with the end of the hose in the water to prevent its swinging. This has proven effective in preventing hose damage. A valve at the end of the hose prevents spillage.

The ALP is designed to function as an unmanned facility, but it is fitted with temporary living accommodations for use by maintenance crews.

The water depth for the ALP in the Beryl Field is about 380 ft. Another ALP, in about 480-ft depth, has been in service since mid-1979 in the Statfjord Field. The Beryl ALP is fitted with a 16-inch diameter loading hose, the Statfjord ALP with a 20-inch hose. Maximum loading rates are about 40,000 and 60,000 barrels per hour, respectively. Year-round operation of these two facilities has shown the ALP configuration to be effective for large volume transportation in severe weather conditions. Tanker loadings can be carried out in wave heights of about 30 ft (9 m) maximum. A second ALP is under construction for the Statfjord Field and another is on order for Beryl.

The SPAR, in the Brent Field, is another concept first used in 1976. In addition to being a loading facility, the Brent SPAR was designed as a storage vessel and pumping station.[3] To make this additional capability possible, the SPAR was arranged to be manned continuously. Its storage capacity is about 300,000 barrels of oil, and the significance of the storage will be discussed later in this chapter. The SPAR is a long, vertical floating cylinder, anchored by six anchor chains. At the top is a turntable fitted with a hose crane which can be swung inboard over the deck of the SPAR for inspection and maintenance of the hoses. The mooring line is connected to the turntable near the base of the hose crane. A helicopter deck on the turntable is about 100 ft above waterline. The SPAR receives oil from a subsea pipe line via submarine hoses. The oil can either pass into the storage tanks or through the SPAR to a tanker via the loading hose. Stored oil is pumped from the SPAR to the tanker. Oil from the Brent Field is now transported by pipe line, so the SPAR acts as a standby unit. However, when fully used, the SPAR has demonstrated its capabilities for year-round operation.

A deep-water SALM was employed in the northern North Sea in 1978. In a water depth of about 520 ft, this unit was used in the Thistle Field[4] during construction of the pipeline. The Thistle SALM employs a rigid column instead of the mooring chain used on the previous SALM designs. The column is connected to a weighted base by a universal joint. An upper universal joint, located at about one-third of the water depth, serves to reduce bending moments in the column. The swivel is fitted just above the upper universal joint, the loading hose is connected just above the swivel. Therefore, as with the shallow-water SALM's, the buoy-end of the hose is submerged, with the part near tanker floating on the surface. The mooring hawser is connected to the top of the SALM, which projects slightly above the surface of the sea. The SALM was used for about nine months before the Thistle pipeline was completed and later was used for stand-by service.

Storage Vessels

The Thistle SALM configuration proved itself well suited to accom-modating high mooring loads in deep water. The Hondo Offshore Storage and Treating Facility, which has just begun operation off California, is a permanently moored production/storage tanker with a SALM as a basic component of its mooring system, similar to the unit shown in Figure 6-4.

The installation of floating storage facilities can be expected in many future offshore developments, because storage is vital to the efficiency of a transportation system that utilizes offshore loading. In severe-weather regions, the storage permits oil production during storms that would prevent the loading of tankers. In addition to the Hondo installation, several permanently moored tankers are currently in service as storage facilities or as combined production and storage facilities. Thus far, all are located in relatively mild-weather areas. However, a storage tanker is being installed this summer in the Fulmar Field in the North Sea. This will introduce a new type of offshore loading system to the North Sea since offtake vessels will moor in tandem to the stern of the storage vessel.

In some heavy-weather areas, the motions of a ship-shaped tanker may cause problems either during storms or during loading operations. Because of this, several low-motion heavy-weather storage/mooring vessel designs have been proposed in recent years.

The Loading Mooring Storage Vessel (LMS), shown in Figure 6-5, which Mobil Shipping and Transportation Co. has been developing,

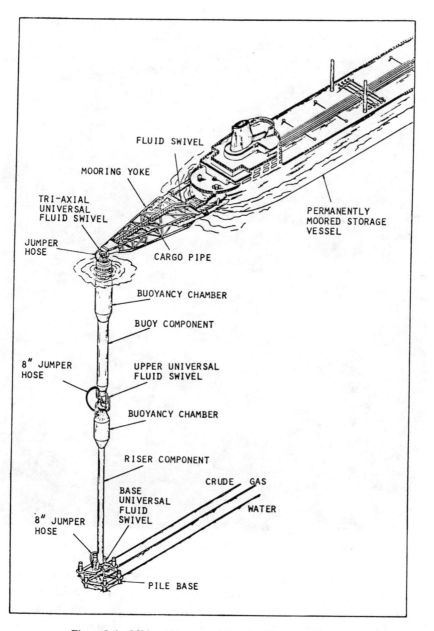

Figure 6-4. Offshore Storage and Treating Facility with SALM.

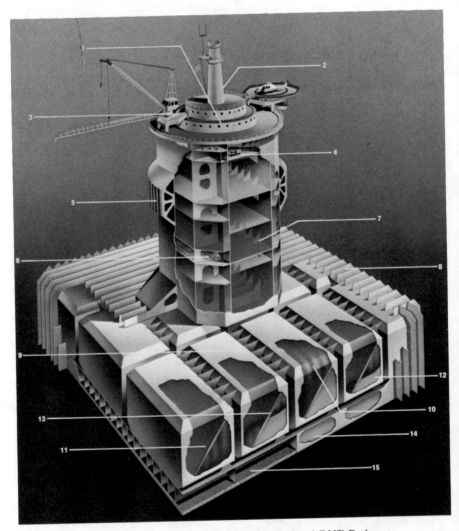

Figure 6-5. Basic Loading Mooring Storage Vessel (LMS) Design.

would comprise a large square box, submerged, with a hexagonal tower projecting above the water's surface. The box would be fitted with 15 dual tanks. These tanks would contain cargo oil, ballast water, or a combination of the two. Nylon-reinforced rubber diaphragms would separate the water and the oil. If a diaphragm were to fail, the ballast water would be passed through oil/water separators to assure clean discharge before being pumped overboard.

The tower would contain cargo tanks, sized so that the difference in density between oil and water in the dual tanks would be compensated for by the oil in the tower when a full cargo was on board. The total cargo capacity would be about 1-1/2 million barrels. Cargo oil would flow from a subsea pipeline via submarine hoses into the LMS. It would be discharged via a crane and loading hose to the offtake tanker. The crane would be mounted on a circular track to permit tankers to be loaded in any downwind position. The mooring hawser would be connected below the crane. The purpose of the small waterplane of the LMS, also in similar designs that have been proposed, is to minimize motions both during the loading of tankers and under storm conditions. These advantages are especially valuable in areas with extremely severe weather.

Other offshore loading designs, both with and without storage, are under development for very deep water and for fields with pack ice and icebergs. Future offshore fields will therefore have many advanced designs from which to choose the most suitable for the specific conditions.

Offtake Vessels

The tankers used in offshore loading service have been fitted with varying amounts of specialized equipment. Opinions differ among companies and individuals on this subject since it is difficult to quantify the benefits of some equipment, but the tendency is to add more sophistication for larger fields, where the penalty for inefficiency is greater.

At the time of startup, the Beryl Field was the largest in the North Sea to use offshore loading as a permanent transportation system. Consequently, the tankers incorporated more specialized features than the tankers used in previous fields. The Beryl tanker equipment includes the following: a bow thruster, specialized bow loading and mooring equipment; and a bow control house, with controls for propeller, thruster, rudder, mooring winches, hawser and hose handling equipment, and the emergency stoppage of production platform pumps, as well as hawser tension monitoring and recording equipment, high pressure alarms, and various other kinds of navigation and communication equipment.

At Statfjord, a larger field, tankers have also been fitted with stern thrusters and proportionately larger bow thrusters. Future offtake vessels may include dynamic positioning equipment, automatic approach control, and additional thrusters.

FACTORS FAVORING OFFSHORE LOADING

The factors that influence the selection of a transportation system are safety, economy, flexibility, and reliability. Offshore loading of oil must also be judged on these criteria.

Safety

Surprising at it may seem, offshore loading can be safer than a pipeline in terms of tanker operation. A fact not always recognized is that crude oil transportation remains incomplete until the oil is delivered to refineries. A pipeline from an offshore field will often terminate in a tank farm, from which the oil must subsequently be transported to tankers. The decision then will not be whether to use marine transportation, but rather where to load the tankers — offshore or in a harbor.

In this context, offshore loading enjoys some inherent safety advantages: (1) the reduction of harbor congestion reduces the risk of collisions; (2) the remoteness from land helps to protect the environment in the event of a tanker mishap during loading; (3) tankers fitted for offshore loading are usually dedicated to that activity, and personnel, therefore, tend to be more familiar with routine and emergency procedures.

Economics

A pipeline may require marine transportation as an integral part of its distribution system. Since both a pipeline and offshore loading incur the cost of acquiring and operating tankers, the comparison between offshore loading and pipe line transportation is essentially reduced to the storage vessel and mooring-loading equipment vs. the pipeline and terminal facilities. And if the production platform provides adequate storage, a buoy can be substituted for the storage vessel. It is easily seen that cost comparisons would strongly favor offshore loading.

Interest rates can also significantly affect the economics of offshore loading vs. pipeline transportation. Pipelines are capital-intensive, especially if new terminal facilities must be constructed on shore, and, therefore, are less attractive when the cost of money is high. In addition, cash flow tends to favor offshore loading. When a field is remote from shore, offshore loading can usually be put into operation faster than a pipe line. This permits earlier generation of income to offset the investment costs. Obviously, where offshore loading has been implemented as a startup system, as it has been in several North Sea fields, the incremental cost to expand to a permanent offshore loading system may be considerably lower than to install a pipeline.

Flexibility

In addition to accommodating the expected variations in the oil production profile, an offshore loading system can cope with unexpected changes in capacity — both increases and decreases. These changes could result from the discovery of additional reservoirs in the vicinity, improved production techniques, a modification of economic conditions, or legislative amendments.

An offshore loading system can also accommodate technological improvements, since obsolescent components can be replaced at relatively low cost. The components of an offshore loading system, which are removed because of reduced economic demand or technological obsolescence, can often be used elsewhere, especially since the offtake vessels could trade in conventional tanker service.

Reliability

Breakdowns can occur with any mechanical equipment. Although an offshore loading system may be more vulnerable to breakdowns than a pipe line, the consequences could be less serious than a pipeline failure. Using backup equipment, an offshore loading system can often continue to function at a reduced rate. However, a pipeline failure can result in complete shutdown of production for an extended period.

The above considerations have necessarily been drawn in abstract terms. For each offshore field under development, the specific factors must be quantified as accurately as possible to permit an objective comparison of offshore loading to pipeline transportation. Nevertheless, the following conditions would tend to favor offshore loading: (1) the distribution of crude oil among several shore sites; (2) the existence of storage capacity in production platforms; (3) high interest rates; (4) uneven or uncertain production profiles, or insufficient production to justify a pipeline; (5) uncertain economic climate; (6) remoteness of the field from shore, or other factors that can delay completion of a pipeline; and (7) the necessity for a "startup" offshore loading system for the pipeline alternative.

EVALUATION OF OFFSHORE LOADING SYSTEMS COMPONENTS

Once a specific offshore loading facility has been proposed, its characteristics must be fully evaluated to determine its operating limitations and to determine whether design improvements are necessary. The two most important considerations are the integrity of the structure and the suitability of the mooring system.

Structure

The first requirement is assurance that the system can survive the maximum 100-year storm conditions. Model tests are most often used to indicate design loads for the system. Equally important for the survivability of the system, however, is fatigue. In this regard, a statistical analysis of the expected cyclical loading on the system is made and applied in conjunction with calculated stress concentration factors for the most critical components to determine the fatigue properties of the structure. If it is found that either the maximum loads or the cyclical loads can cause structural damage, the system must be redesigned and reanalyzed.

Mooring Hawser

Once the soundness of the structure has been confirmed, the determination of its operating limits can begin. In most offshore loading systems, the limitation on operations is hawser tension. Most systems in the North Sea, using 21-inch circumference nylon hawsers, work to a tension limit of between 100 and 200 tons, depending upon the particular configuration and the operator's policy. Model tests are run to determine what weather conditions would create excessive tensions. In actual practice, the limiting operating conditions vary considerably, dependent upon wave height and period, wind speed and direction, and current speed and direction. Usually, due to the limitations of model test facilities, only a few conditions can be tested and a rough estimate established for the operating limits. Therefore, computer motion simulation programs are often used to model the system. With these programs, the effects of many more variations of wind, wave, and current can be determined.

From this testing, the designer can determine a reasonable set of operating limits for the mooring system, which can then be used to evaluate the performance of the transportation system as discussed below. If the system performance is found to be below expectations, the entire storage, loading, and marine transportation system might be redesigned.

OVERALL PERFORMANCE OF OFFSHORE LOADING SYSTEMS

The measure of performance used to evaluate an offshore storage, loading, and marine transportation system is "transportation efficiency." This is the amount of crude oil produced and delivered to shore as a percentage of the amount that could have been produced and moved by a perfect transportation system. An example of a perfect, 100% efficient transportation system would be a pipeline with no breakdown.

For calculating efficiency, an offshore loading simulation program, originally developed by Mobil Shipping and Transportation Co. in 1973 to evaluate offshore loading for the Beryl Field, can be used. This computer program has been expanded over the years to permit more complex evaluations, and it provides the capability to analyze the effects on transportation efficiency of variations in the following parameters: (1) production rates, (2) storage volumes in the production platforms and in the SPM's, (3) number and characteristics of ships, (4) voyage distance; (5) safe mooring and loading wave height limitations, (6) number of SPM's, (7) breakdown frequencies and repair time for SPM's, (8) loading rate, and (9) weather data.

In reality, the environmental limitations are complex, but this simulation utilizes wave height as the sole criterion to decide whether a ship can moor or whether a moored ship must cast off. Despite this simplification, use of the program in evaluating Beryl and Statfjord Fields has given good estimates of transportation efficiency. The simulation has been used for doing sensitivity studies on storage at the field, number and sizes of ships, number and types of SPM's and off-loading rates in order to define the most economical offshore loading system. Essentially, the program uses wave height data recorded on or near the offshore loading site, and simulates events in three-hour increments for up to twenty years.

A sample run was made in which a five-year set of actual wave height measurements was used, to which other input parameters, fictitious, but nevertheless representative of activities in a typical field in the North Sea, were added. In this run "significant" wave height, which is the average of the highest one-third of all waves over a given period of time, was used rather than maximum wave height, which would be almost twice the significant height. This program allows an analysis of the overall utilization of the ships and SPM's and provides a daily listing of production cutbacks. In the end, the program shows the average production efficiency for each month of the year with the maximum daily production of a platform and net storage.

Figures 6-6 to 6-8 were developed from a series of program runs of the example. Figure 6-6 shows a plot of transportation efficiency versus storage with excess shipping. As can be seen, storage is necessary to achieve a high level of transportation efficiency. At the same time, it is apparent that there is a point of diminishing returns. In an actual application, economic calculations would also be made to establish the most cost-effective level of storage for the field.

Figure 6-7 shows a plot of transportation efficiency versus maximum mooring and loading wave heights with excess shipping and with available storage equal to six days of production. Here it can be seen that increasing the limiting significant wave height for mooring above 13 ft would have only a minor effect on transportation efficiency for this example.

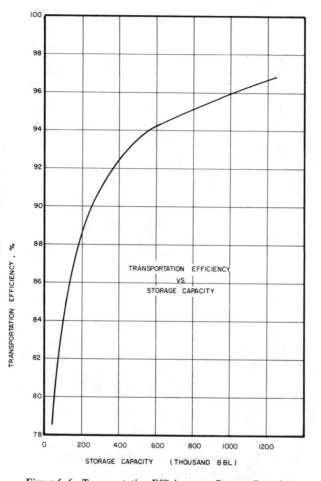

Figure 6-6. Transportation Efficiency vs. Storage Capacity.

Figure 6-8 shows a plot of transportation efficiency versus number of ships. In this case, two ships would be sufficient, a conclusion generated by the sample run, which showed that a third ship would be only occasionally utilized.

Further analyses of the program and its output would show that efficiency is relatively insensitive to variations of other parameters. The total system design, therefore, usually focuses on balancing the

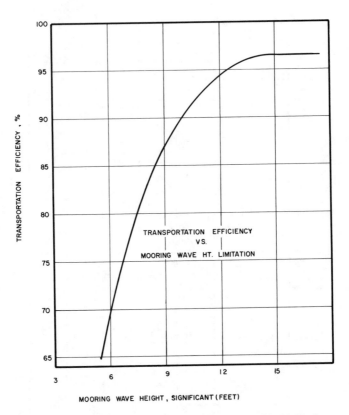

Figure 6-7. Transportation Efficiency vs. Mooring Height Limitation.

storage volume, the wave height limitations, and number of ships needed to achieve the most cost-effective system.

CONCLUSION

The offshore loading of tankers has proven to be not only feasible but also economical, even in severe weather areas like the North Sea. Thus, offshore loading provides an alternative transportation system to a pipe line where either the cost or the time required for building the pipeline might be excessive or where the life or the production profile of the field may make a pipeline uneconomical. Techniques that permit the assessment of performance are available, so that offshore

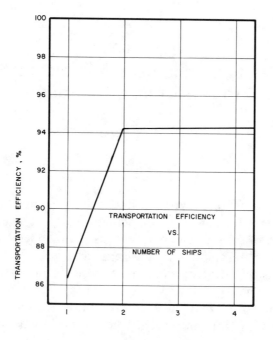

NUMBER OF OFFTAKE VESSEL

Figure 6-8. Transportation Efficiency vs. Number of Ships.

loading systems and pipeline systems can be compared on the basis of valid life-cycle economics.

NOTES TO CHAPTER 6

1. Versluis, J., "Exposed Location Single Buoy Mooring," *OTC Proceedings 1980,* OTC Paper 3805.
2. Hays, D.L., McSwiggan, M., and Vilain, R., "Operation of an Articulated Oil Loading Column at the Beryl Field in the North Sea," *OTC Proceedings 1979,* OTC Paper 3563.
3. Bax, J.D., "First SPAR Storage-Loading Buoy Project Posed Complex De-sign, Construction Problem," *Offshore Platforms and Pipelining,* The Petro-leum Publishing Company, Tulsa, 1976.
4. Millar, J.L., Hughes, H., and Dyer, R.C., "First Year's Operation Experi-ence of the Deepest SPM In the World," *OTC Proceedings 1979,* OTC Paper 3561.

Chapter 7
Safety Standards and Accidents in Frontier Drilling Operations

Thomas S. McIntosh

In this time of national hypersensitivity in the United States to matters involving safety and environmental quality, the very raising of the question of the safety of offshore gas and oil operations seems to create a public presumption of negligence and guilt. The offshore gas and oil industry has often found itself in the uncomfortable position of being assumed guilty and forced to prove itself innocent. The facts, instead, show that the offshore industry is up to the task of drilling safely in frontier areas and hostile environments. The basis for this assertion is the current performance of the industry.

A great debate about the exploration and development of the resources of the continental shelf has been raging for years. On one side of the debate stand the critics of the gas and oil industry, who fault offshore safety standards and who specify that increased government regulation and extensive technological changes are needed. On the other side, stands the industry itself, which believes the safety issue is misunderstood; that available statistics have been distorted to give an inaccurate impression, and that improved safety can only come through an approach that stresses a human solution. At the root of this debate is a communications problem. The offshore gas and oil industry is not well understood by outsiders. The industry itself has been largely at fault because it has seldom taken the time to tell its story.

The haze of misinformation and misconception that clouds much thinking about offshore safety must be cleared. The equipment and the procedures are ready to tackle frontier drilling operations; the industry is ready to take on severe environments. The key to safe offshore operations will continue to be experienced personnel trained to stress safety, not new regulations or expensive hardware.

Safety-trained personnel are not something the industry can order like so many tons of drilling mud. Their development requires detailed, often laborious, on-site effort. And it requires something even more basic: a management commitment to view safety as a managed activity, like any other activity in the industry, with whole-hearted support.

Just how dangerous are the operations of the offshore gas and oil industry? Simple questions do not always yield simple answers. First, statistics can be misleading. Every industry has a different percentage of individuals exposed to harm. In the offshore gas and oil industry, for example, a very large percentage of employees work on drilling rigs; in some companies that rate stands near 95 percent. It can be misleading to compare the offshore industry with other industries, unless that industry has a similar ratio of persons actually exposed to industrial accidents. An industry that has 40 percent of its employees in administrative functions in offices will show a lower accident frequency than one with 95 percent of its workers in manufacturing, transportation, construction, and production functions.

The offshore gas and oil industry also has a high personnel turnover – often more than 100 percent a year. This means a short time on the job and a correspondingly brief exposure to training at a specific site. The turnover situation is worse today because the offshore industry is in a state of unprecedented expansion. As a consequence, personnel are being added at a prodigious rate. In many cases, experienced personnel have been spread thinner than the industry would like. Where there are substantial numbers of new workers, the problem of safety is greater than when the work force is more experienced.

But clearly the problems are mostly "people problems," not technological ones.

Statistical concerns notwithstanding, some conclusions can be drawn about the safety of offshore operations from a report issued in May 1981 by the National Research Council. Entitled *Safety and Offshore Oil,* the study did not plow a great deal of new ground, but it did present an informative compilation of information on outer continental shelf activities. To quote from the report: "The frequency of injuries on oil and gas operations on the outer continental shelf is comparable to that of other industries, such as mining, maritime transportation, and heavy construction . . . "[1] The report also noted that workplace safety on the outer continental shelf was an area of concern, "but not one easily improved by legislation or detailed regulation. Work on the outer continental shelf appeared to be no more hazardous than in similar industries ashore."[2]

The offshore industry has, in fact, shown a downward trend in the incidence of disabling injuries during the last decade. Since 1973, the frequency of disabling accidents has fallen more than 20 percent, as shown in Table 7-1, yet during the same period the number of hours worked has increased nearly 150 percent. Why, then, is the offshore industry considered an unsafe or unusually hazardous industry? In large part, this is a result of the "airplane syndrome." There is a widely-held belief that air travel is a dangerous business when, in fact, airline travel is safer than taking a car out for a drive on the highways.

The difference is that auto accidents involve small numbers of people and generally receive only local attention. When an airliner goes down it is a dramatic catastrophe involving a large number of lives and receives international news coverage.

The same is true of the offshore drilling industry. One accident last year alone caused more than one-third of the 331 deaths reported

Table 7-1. Frequency of Lost-Time Accidents (U.S. Offshore).

YEAR	TOTAL MAN-HOURS	INJURIES	FREQUENCY[b]
1973	15,313,919	797	52.04
1974	3,883,462[a]	782	49.96
1975	18,663,520	781	41.85
1976	18,184,585	1,076	59.17
1977	28,834,239	1,343	46.57
1978	36,173,267	1,797	49.68
1979	36,043,946	1,646	45.66
1980	37,077,474	1,518	40.94
1981	43,599,535	1,485	34.06

Source: International Association of Drilling Contractors

[a] 1st Quarter only

[b] Accident frequency is lost-time accidents multiplied by 1,000,000 and divided by man-hours of work.

Table 7-2. Number of Lives Lost in Structural Accidents of Mobile Platforms Worldwide, 1970–1980.

INITIATING EVENT	TOTAL	STRUCTURAL LOSS			NONE	TOTAL LIVES LOST
		SEVERE	DAMAGE	MINOR		
Weather	13					13
Collision	1	8		4		13
Blowout	5	26	20			51
Leakage		1				1
Machine, etc.			1			1
Fire						0
Explosion		2	2	8		12
Foundering			1			1
Grounding		6				6
Capsizing	93	6	1			100
Structural strength	123 (*Kielland*)			7	1	131
Other				2		2
TOTALS	235	49	25	21	1	331

Source: "Lloyd's List"

as a result of mobile rig accidents during the entire decade of the 1970s, as shown in Table 7-2. Put another way, this single accident, which may never be repeated again, caused a jump of more than 50 percent in the fatality rate for the entire decade. Clearly such an event skews the mean significantly and leaves a wrong impression about the safety of offshore operations. Yet such a dramatic incident has been responsible for much of the clamor to impose more stringent safety regulations and revise technology aboard the world's offshore drilling rigs.

The accident in 1980 that caused the clamor about the safety of offshore operations was the capsizing of the *Alexander L. Kielland.* The *Kielland* incident provides an excellent case study, for it shows that improving the safety of the offshore industry is not entirely or even principally a technical problem. It is primarily a task of training personnel.

The *Alexander L. Kielland* was a mobile platform that had five supporting pontoons arranged in a pentagon pattern. The *Kielland* was built as a drilling rig, but its Norwegian owners never used it for that purpose. Since it was delivered in 1976, the *Kielland* had served as an accommodation platform, or "floatel." Its original capacity was only 80 beds, but its accommodations had been expanded to include 348 beds.

The five columns that served as pontoons for the platform were supported by a series of bracings. The weakness in this system was caused by the location of a hydrophone that had been welded to one of the bracings. This was a critical error, and it was a human error. The welds were not as good as they could have been, and resulted in the fracturing of the steel in the bracing. The high stress from waves and wind in the severe environment of the North Sea further cracked and fatigued the metal in the bracing.

On 27 March 1980, at about 6:00 P.M., the *Kielland* lay at anchor in the Ekofisk field, close to production platform Edda 1/7C. It had been in this vicinity for about nine months. The weather was rough, with high winds and waves running to more than 30 ft. The stress was too much for the defective bracing and it parted. The redistribution of stress overloaded the five other bracings that connected one of the five floatation columns to the platform. When they failed, the column broke away entirely. With that column gone, the *Kielland* immediately heeled over about 35 degrees and temporarily stabilized. It continued to heel over and to sink, however, and in 20 minutes it turned upside down. Of the 212 men on board, 123 lost their lives.

What caused this tragedy? Design problems were a contributing factor, but they were made much worse by human error both before and after the rig was built. No evaluation of the resistance against fatigue failure had been made of the actual structural component involved, in spite of the fact that applicable construction codes contained such requirements. Not only was the placement of the hydrophone unfortunate, but the weld was also inadequate.

Norway is legendary for probably having the strictest set of offshore rig regulations in the western world. As a consequence, the *Kielland* was inspected under the most stringent international principles then known — and passed those tests. According to Professor Torgeir Moan, a member of the Royal Norwegian commission appointed to investigate the *Kielland* accident, the cracks originated during construction.[3] The rig was inspected both in the shipyard and in operation, yet in both cases the inspectors missed the fatal cracks caused by the hydrophone welds.

Design and technical problems augmented by human error explain why the *Kielland* capsized, but they do not wholly account for the high loss of life in the accident. Of the 212 men on the platform at the time of the mishap only a handful had significant offshore experience or had apparently received the safety orientation and training in use by most U.S. companies, and which has long been advocated by the International Association of Drilling Contractors (IADC).

The floatel guests were primarily construction workers, not rig-trained personnel. They had little or no experience or training in offshore safety procedures. They were unfamiliar with abandon ship procedures and survival tactics in the icy environment of the North Sea. When the *Kielland* heeled over, panic ensured. Men rushed to the lifeboat stations. Few took time to get life jackets. Safety training would have produced a more disciplined movement to the lifeboats. Because of the list of the *Kielland,* the lifeboat hooks were difficult to release. Three of the boats were blown against the platform and crushed. Another lifeboat came down upside down. Only two of seven lifeboats on the rig were successfully launched. The *Kielland* had a 200 percent lifeboat capacity, but panic prevented its proper use. A safety-trained crew would have been conditioned to follow the orders of the person in charge of a lifeboat, and quickly move to other lifeboat stations as needed.

The men who were living aboard the *Kielland* were in one of the more hostile marine environments in the world. Yet they were virtually without safety orientation and training; without a clear idea of what they should do in case of an emergency. Throughout this story one point rings clear: Equipment malfunction may have been the catalyst of the accident, but it was human failure that made the accident a tragedy.

The IADC issues what it calls the "Charlie Report" every year. This report details injury statistics for both the onshore and offshore drilling industries. In the 1980 Charlie Report, the causes were reported for a total of 1,049 lost-time accidents in U.S. waters, as shown in Table 7-3. Of these, 754 (more than 70 percent) were attributed to "unsafe acts" rather than "unsafe conditions." In foreign waters, 50 of 69 reported lost-time accidents were attributed to unsafe acts.[4]

Table 7-3. 1980 Offshore Accident Facts.

U.S. WATERS			
Cause of Accident			*Number*
Unsafe Act			754
Unsafe Condition			228
Other			67
FOREIGN WATERS			
Cause of Accident			*Number*
Unsafe Act			50
Unsafe Condition			17
Other			2
FREQUENCY*	1980	1979	Decrease
U.S. Water	40.94	45.66	4.72
U.S. Land	57.76	58.08	0.32

*Lost-time accidents per million man-hours.
Source: 1980 "Charlie Report," International Association of Drilling Contractors

Parenthetically, the IADC lists an accident as lost-time if the worker is off the job more than 12 hours. The U.S. Coast Guard, by contrast, does not log a maritime accident until the worker has been off the job 72 hours.

The Zapata Offshore Company has found that there is a direct correlation between on-the-job experience and decreasing accident frequency. This is one reason why new Zapata employees begin intensive safety training the moment they set foot on the rig. The company knows this approach works; since Zapata initiated its safety program in 1977, lost-time accidents have been cut by 65 percent. Downtime due to equipment failures was also reduced by 30 percent. Furthermore, employee attrition — always a problem in industry — has decreased from more than 100 percent a year in 1977 to about 50 percent in 1981.

Behind all of the Zapata safety and training programs, behind the more than two million dollars a year that the company has spent on such programs, is a deep and practical conviction that preventing accidents and developing people's skills has a direct positive effect on the company's profitability. The key to a successful safety program is solid management commitment. Too often safety, not just in offshore drilling but in many industries, has been viewed as an appendage to production, a nicety to make the insurance companies happy, a formal program operating in a vacuum without meaningful support or result.

Safety training must be viewed as a vital management function, as essential to the business as recruitment of personnel, maintenance of inventory, or management of cash flow. Safety must be a production-oriented process in which the product is safety-trained personnel. A safer workplace means reduced downtime, reduced medical and insurance costs, and better company acceptance in the marketplace.

At Zapata, the commitment to safety extends to the top levels of management. Among other things the program includes regular meetings of the Accident Prevention Review Board. Chaired by the Senior Vice President for Operations, this panel reviews accidents and insures that corrective action is taken. Safe Plan of Action Awards are made to emphasize the importance of having a definite plan for safety in all situations.

At the rig level, the key operative in Zapata's safety program is the Rig Safety and Training Representative, usually known as the RSTR. RSTRs provide full-time, rig-based safety training as well as administrative and employee relations assistance to the crews. Zapata's RSTRs are themselves trained to provide emergency medical treatment (many served as medical corpsmen in the Armed Forces), but their primary responsibility is accident prevention. The RSTR is one of the first people a new employee meets when he or she sets foot on a Zapata rig. The crew member will see him again and again – on the drill floor, by the mud pits, and at rig safety and training seminars. The RSTR becomes a trusted counselor to the rig crew because they know he is there for their support and well-being.

Zapata's safety and training programs reduce downtime, and that reduces costs. But they are also morale builders because they are "people programs." They build a feeling of belonging, of being a proud part of a highly successful operation. When an employee takes pride in the job, he or she will take extra care to be efficient and productive. This is important in today's drilling industry; the industry has changed in the last 20 years, and so have its workers. Today, there is a better educated, more sophisticated work force than 20 or even 10 years ago. It is a work force less tolerant of harsh environments than its predecessors. Today, the industry has to compete with land-based jobs that are cleaner, have regular hours, and perhaps more glamour. The industry is also competing for a rapidly dwindling labor supply. The post-World War II "baby boom" is over, and the 18–26 year old age group is shrinking.

Compensation is one way to make offshore work attractive, but it is not enough. The work place must be made safer and the job less strenuous, while the company strives to build that all-important esprit de corps. Once again, safety and training programs can play a key role among the tools of management. Zapata's personnel turnover is quite low within the industry, and credit must be given to the safety and training programs.

There is a bonus to the safety program that extends beyond safety or morale building. The infrastructure of the program – its management commitment, the communications network, and the implementation procedures – can be used effectively to manage other areas on the rig. Job evaluation, monitoring the marine condition of the vessel, and inventory control are three of the areas that are responding favorably to the management system that was first built for the safety and training programs.

When Zapata initiated its safety program in its present form, it was the first in the industry. But it was quickly copied by other companies, which was not only a vote of confidence for that approach, but also one more illustration of the continuing concern for safety in the offshore gas and oil industry.

When the IADC's predecessor organization was founded in 1940, a Safety Committee was one of the first units to be organized. The IADC in 1981 was sponsoring work in 20 schools to insure that the organization's membership would be kept current on the latest in personnel development techniques. In 1980, nearly 8,400 persons took such course work.

The efforts of Zapata and the IADC have been cited as examples of the strong safety consciousness of the offshore industry. Technology is not a restricting factor in challenging the frontier oceans of the world. Its progress has been steady and rewarding. A number of recent technological advances, such as better pipe-handling equipment, computer technology, and satellite navigation, have combined to make the offshore job easier than it was a decade ago. The industry has been quick to utilize technological breakthroughs, not because of government regulations, but because it must do so to stay competitive and to effectively meet the challenge of increasingly difficult environments offshore. The industry's efficient and effective equipment and training methods have evolved because of the difficulties of confronting real production problems with finite resources. Few, if any, have appeared as a result of government regulations.

A National Research Council study has spoken to the issue of safety and offshore oil. The Council's Committee on Assessment of Safety of OCS Activities found no evidence that more hostile physical environments or more difficult operations, by themselves, led to more accidents. The Committee, however, felt that there may be a need for special measures, such as protective gear, general procedures, training supervision, and personnel selection: "The knowledge required to insure workplace safety in extreme environments is already in hand in the cumulative experience of the oil industry and the military services. There is no evidence that additional regulations regarding workplace safety are needed for frontier areas, nor that major developments in workplace safety technology are indicated."[5]

Nevertheless, when a dramatic tragedy such as the *Kielland* disaster focuses government and public attention on the drilling industry, the inevitable cry is for more regulation. But other industries, such as coal mining, which are highly regulated, have accident records worse than the offshore gas and oil industry. The offshore industry has not been without oversight. It is already subject to numerous federal safety regulations while operating on this nation's outer continental shelf. But our experience has led us to question whether detailed government regulations actually improve safety.

That skepticism about government regulation was deepened recently by an incident in the Gulf of Mexico. Two Coast Guard inspectors went aboard an old submersible rig and proceeded to write a record 188 citations for failures to comply with Coast Guard safety regulations. It was only after the inspection was over — and the citations written — that the Coast Guard discovered that of all the rigs in that owner's fleet, the old submersible has the best safety record. In fact, there had not been a lost-time accident on that rig for two years.

A strong argument can be made that the foundation of improved offshore safety will rest neither on increased public regulation nor on technological improvements. People are the solution to accident prevention. When safety programs are given the commitment of management and executed as a vital part of the overall business operation, the results can be outstanding. The offshore drilling industry believes it has achieved a level of "acceptable risk." The record of four decades clearly shows the offshore industry's commitment to providing the safest possible working conditions, and it is ready to meet the challenges of producing gas and oil in the world's frontier offshore areas.

NOTES TO CHAPTER 7

1. *Safety and Offshore Oil,* Committee on Assessment of OCS Activities, Marine Board, Assembly of Engineering, National Research Council, National Academy of Sciences, Washington, D.C., p. 136.
2. Ibid., p. 14.
3. "The *Alexander L. Kielland* Accident," Torgeir Moan, Professor of Marine Studies, the Norwegian Institute of Technology, Trondheim, Norway, p. 6.
4. "Charlie Report for 1980," Accident Prevention Committee of 1980, International Association of Drilling Contractors, Houston, Texas, pp. 16 and 19.
5. *Safety and Offshore Oil,* Committee on Assessment of Safety of OCS Activities, Marine Board, Assembly of Engineering, National Research Council, National Academy of Sciences, Washington, D.C., p. 15.

Chapter 8
Workplace Safety Problems in Offshore Operations

Lawrence R. Zeitlin

Injury and death of personnel can occur in the course of the exploration and exploitation of gas and oil from offshore areas. Based on current IADC statistics, a death or disabling injury will occur for each ten man-years worked on a gas or oil drilling rig. Although there has been a gradual decline in accident rates over the last few years, the absolute number of deaths and injuries, and their attendant costs, has risen sharply. The drain on human and financial resources is a point of concern to all sectors of the industry.

Why is the accident rate so high? Clearly the occupation has elements of danger, but is work on a drilling rig inherently more dangerous than in construction of other industries? Need special precautions be taken to assure the safety of offshore workplaces in frontier areas? If this were a shoreside industry, say shipbuilding or coal mining, it might be possible to answer those questions unambiguously by reference to a single body of information, such as that maintained by OSHA or the Bureau of Labor Statistics. Unfortunately there is no single body of data covering the offshore oil industry. Rather there are multiple partial bodies of data impinging on the problem of workplace safety, collected by a variety of agencies, domestic and foreign, for different purposes. Reporting populations, exposure periods, and even the definition of injury differ so substantially across data bases that direct comparison between industries, or even within sectors of the petroleum industry, becomes difficult. By appropriate selections from data it is possible to show that gas and oil drilling offshore is safer or more dangerous than drilling on land; that construction or heavy industry is safer or more dangerous than offshore drilling.

Death, however, is unambiguous. It is only in the reporting of fatalities that the various data collecting agencies are in general agreement. After reviewing all relevant data sources, the National Research Council Committee on the Assessment of Safety of Outer Continental Shelf Activities finally abandoned efforts to quantify workplace hazards in the offshore drilling industry. It reached the general conclusion that:

> . . . oil and gas activities on the outer continental shelf of the United States are fairly dangerous, but not so much as might be expected from the nature of the work performed and the characteristics of the workplace. Oil and gas activities on the outer continental shelf appear to be less dangerous than construction and about as safe as general manufacturing.[1]

The Norwegians, on the other hand, with a body of data based on North Sea experience, and a death and injury rate almost twice that occuring on the U.S. Outer Continental Shelf, concluded that offshore work was approximately as risky as metal mining, traditionally one of the more dangerous industrial activities.

Thus the workplace safety differences between the relatively benign U.S. Outer Continental Shelf and the frontierlike North Sea can be compared to the difference between general manufacturing and metal mining. And that, regrettably, is about as far as analysis of the *current* industry wide personal injury data base can go. The following comments then, are based on a soft, rather than a hard, analysis of the aforementioned data, and a quarter of a century of experience in industrial and maritime safety. The analysis relies primarily on fatality data as an index of comparative workplace safety, using American, British, and Norwegian North Sea experience to model the frontier environment, and U.S. data from the outer continental shelf in the Gulf of Mexico as the model for a mature developed area.

THE NATURE OF WORKPLACE SAFETY

Workplace safety can be broadly defined as the probability that a given workplace is free from *unexpected* or *unanticipated* agents or situations that can cause harm to a *trained worker* carrying out the *proper functions* of his job. Any workplace accident involves an interaction between a susceptible individual, a hazardous environment or equipment, and an injury-producing agent. This interaction takes place in a situation in which unexpected, unavoidable, or unintentional aspects of the physical environment, in combination with various aspects of the individual's behavior, result in injury to the individual (or others) and/or the damage of equipment.

From this definition, it can be seen that few workplace accidents are really "accidents" in the sense of being purely chance events. Rather accidents consist of that large class of events characterized by low predictability and controllability and having undesirable consequences. Critical to the problem of workplace safety is the reduction of uncertainty and the increase in predictability and control of all phases of workplace activity. If we can anticipate an undesirable situation, we can take precautions against it. The situations that hurt us are those we cannot anticipate.

CHARACTERISTICS OF FRONTIER AREAS

A frontier area is any area in which the industry has less than ten years of drilling experience. The most salient characteristic of a frontier area is uncertainty about the problems to be faced and the methods of coping with them.

From the viewpoint of workplace safety, frontier areas should be characterized not in terms of the extremity of environmental and working conditions but by the lack of knowledge in dealing with them. Ten years experience buys knowledge and, within economic constraints, permits management to deal with the problems. Although the 1980 injury and death rate in the North Sea area was about twice as high as on the U.S. Outer Continental Shelf, it has been declining rapidly. Eight years ago it was four times as high. As a frontier, the North Sea is rapidly being tamed.

THE COMMON FACTOR APPROACH TO ACCIDENT REDUCTION

The workplace accident itself is marked by the combined existence or occurrence of a number of coincidental events and circumstances of a casual nature. In the absence of any one of these, the situation would have been uneventful. A slight change in the behavior of the worker, in the environment, or in the equipment being used is all that would have been necessary to have prevented the accident. Prevention of a specific accident, in hindsight, always seems simple. At the same time, there are countless combination of circumstances that produce accidents. To prevent a substantial number of accidents, it is essential that the condition to be changed, modified, or eliminated by a common factor of many accident situations. General improvements in workplace safety arise directly from the identification of such common factors. Experience points to four aspects of offshore activities in which such common factors may be found: (1) hazardous work activities and equipment; (2) the physical environment; (3) transportation interfaces; and (4) worker characteristics.

HAZARDOUS WORK ACTIVITIES AND EQUIPMENT

Work offshore is divided into three major phases; construction, exploration and development drilling, and production. Each phase has distinct work activities and workplace hazards. As a consequence, the pattern of injuries is different for each phase and the specific actions to improve workplace safety are also different. Table 8-1 summarizes the phases, activities, and hazards of offshore gas and oil operations.

Construction

Construction involves the fabrication and assembly of platforms and other structures on the drilling site. It closely resembles shoreside commercial construction and steel erection in the skills used and in the hazards faced by workers. Both in the United States and the North Sea, falls represent the most common single cause of injury, followed closely be burns from welding equipment and injuries from falling objects. The probability of falls is increased by the partial or complete absence of protected walkways and guard rails, the extensive use of scaffolding and temporary construction, and the use of unsecured vertical ladders. Falls into the sea or to a lower level are common because of incomplete decking. Movement of heavy structures by cranes involves hazards of rope breakage or load shifting. Despite the danger inherent in construction, there is little evidence that the hazards offshore are any greater than those on land. Further, the appreciation of the obvious dangers of

Table 8-1. Workplace Hazards Inherent in Offshore Gas and Oil Operations.

PHASE	NATURE OF ACTIVITY	HUMAN FUNCTIONS IN WORKPLACE	RELATED INDUSTRIES	PROBABLE SAFETY HAZARDS	INJURY TYPES	PREVENTIVE ACTIONS
CONSTRUCTION	Fabrication and/or assembly of structures on site. Installation of drill rigs. Removal of structures.	Activities related to steel erection; welding; cutting; assembly. Heavy lift crane operations. Diving.	Commercial construction. Bridge and tunnel construction. Shipbuilding.	FALLS – most frequent cause of injury. Falling objects. Exposure to weather extremes. Welding, cutting hazards. Poorly secured scaffolds. Crane and rope failure.	Death, fractures from falls. Drowning. Welding burns. Contusions, sprains, strains, abrasions. Crushing from crane accidents.	Early installation of guard rails, nets. Safety harnesses. Protective helmets and clothing. Man overboard recovery systems. Crane inspection and cable renewal. Safety training of contract personnel.
DRILLING AND WORKOVER	Drilling, logging, fishing. Setting casing. Cementing. Completion. Workover operations.	Manhandling drill string during tripping. Moving casing, setting. Placing and withdrawing instruments. Cementing. Control of well during drilling. Blowout diagnosis and prevention. Hoist and crane operations.	Land based drilling. Heavy equipment assembly. Foundry work.	STRUCK BY OBJECTS – most frequent form of injury. Falls. Slippery drill floors. Rotating equipment. Crushing between objects. Exposure, fatigue, long shifts. Blowouts (infrequent). Crane load shifts.	Injury to extremities. Contusions, abrasions, crushing. Sprains and strains from moving heavy equipment. Fractures from falls.	Drill floor housekeeping. Proper training of drilling team. "Iron roughnecks" Guard rails, deck opening barriers. Training in blowout prevention. Personnel selection. Safety training.
PRODUCTION	Control of product flow from well. Degassing. Equipment maintenance. Production record keeping. Well maintenance.	Monitoring well status. Control of well output. Record keeping. Maintenance.	Process control industries. Chemical plant. Refinery.	FALLS – between levels. Fire. High pressure systems. Crane operations by unqualified persons.	Fractures. Burns. Struck by falling object.	Proper training in maintenance procedures. Safety training. Fire control equipment. Fire control training.

"high steel" work tends to promote an awareness of safety on the part of the individual worker that is lacking in other phases of operation.

The increased hazards of environmental extremes encountered in some frontier areas tends to be compensated by the fact that in these areas significant portions of the structure are completed near shore or in shipyards and then towed to the drilling location. This has the effect of decreasing the number of workplace injuries at the offshore location by deferring them to the shoreside construction facility.

The relative maturity of the field also influences the injury and fatality rate experienced during the construction phase. In the Gulf of Mexico, for example, construction accounts for only 1.1% of all offshore fatalities while in the North Sea the rate is 13.4%. On a per capita basis, the accident rate is almost the same in both areas, the lower overall percentage in the Gulf being due to the smaller proportion of personnel involved in construction.

Drilling

All activities necessary to drill the hole and install casing can be subsumed under drilling. It takes place in exploration, appraisal, and development phases of outer continental shelf activities. Drilling is a labor intensive operation and requires the handling of drills, drill pipe, casing, and other heavy pieces of equipment. The drill floor is undoubtedly a dangerous place in which to work. The surfaces are often slippery from rain and drilling mud. Work takes place in the open, unprotected from temperature and weather extremes. Drilling is a 24 hour activity and shifts are often as long as 12 hours.

The most common cause of injury during drilling results from being struck by a moving object, being caught between objects, or being crushed between an object and the rig structure. A few minutes observation of a drilling crew at work will show why this is so. When pipe is being tripped in or out of a hole, the crew moves with the precision of a Super Bowl backfield. A momentary misstep, a slip on a muddy floor, a hand out of place, and the crew member is likely to be injured. Tongs represent the single piece of equipment most likely to cause injury on the drilling floor, accounting for nearly a third of all casualties. Falls represent the next major source of injury.

Drilling is clearly the most dangerous work activity offshore. In the Gulf of Mexico, 55.6% of fatalities occurred during this phase, while in the North Sea the rate was 74.3%. Again the disparity in rates can be attributed to the greater percentage of personnel involved in drilling in the North Sea.

Production

The control of the product flow from the well is a function of production. It differs from construction and drilling in that the problems of the workplace are chronic rather than acute. Aside from the ever present danger of falls, the flammable or explosive nature of oil and gas under pressure presents the greatest hazard in the workplace. A survey of the outer continental shelf events file of the U.S. Geological Survey shows a number of injuries resulting from the failure of a pressurized portion of the system. Either the worker was directly injured by the failed component or was burned by the flash fire resulting from the leakage of gas. In many of these incidents, failure to observe safety precautions when working around pressurized systems, for example, while performing maintenance welding, seemed to be a precipitating cause.

The relative safety of production operations is likely to result in an underestimation of the potential hazards of the product. In the United States, the outer continental shelf fatality rate during production is only one-eighth that in drilling. Still, so many workers are engaged in production in U.S. waters that production fatalities account for 41% of all deaths. In the North Sea, production fatalities represent 14.6% of offshore deaths. On the basis of current evidence there does not appear to be a significant increase in personal hazard resulting from work activities in frontier areas. This is as expected since equipments and work procedures are nearly the same as in more mature areas.

Workplace hazards resulting from the physical environment must be divided into those resulting from the man-made structure (the drilling or production platform) and the natural environment. The typical offshore platform, semisubmersible, or jack up rig is a multilevel structure of relatively small area. Operations are carried out on several levels, the crew being required to move from level to level as the job function requires. Decks frequently have access holes to service equipment below deck level. To conserve limited deck space, stairs often have a higher pitch than optimum for safety. The hazard is obvious. Apart from personnel on the drill floor, falls represent the greatest single source of injury in the offshore gas and oil industry.

The closest parallel to a small area, multilevel environment, is found in the shipping industry. Ships share many of the structural features of drilling platforms and here too, falls represent a major source of personnel injuries. There the parallel ends, for while maritime casualties are strongly influenced by the nature of the wind and sea state, most drilling rigs appear to be relatively immune to casualties caused by none-extreme natural phenomena. There are, of course, exceptions. Structural failure under extreme conditions, while rare, has occurred with catastrophic results. Such failures are outside the scope of most considerations of workplace safety.

Unfortunately for the gas and oil industry, most of the areas proposed for future exploitation lie in regions of climatic extremes. Although it is possible for an individual to gain some degree of acclimatization to extremes of heat or cold after several weeks of exposure, there is always some decrement in performance when compared to a more normal environment. Extremes of cold are the easier to deal with since protective clothing can be provided to permit some degree for activity down to temperatures of -40°F. Further, since most work on a drilling rig is of a highly physical nature, the body heat generated is beneficial. The main effect of cold on a healthy individual is to decrease manual dexterity by lessening the sensitivity of the skin to sensations of touch and pressure. Gloves and other protective clothing interfere with the operation of equipment. There is a general agreement among researchers that performance starts to deteriorate when the skin temperature drops below 55°F. Compared to normal "shirtsleeve" conditions, the performance decrement at 30°F is about 20%, at -40°F, the performance decrement is 80%.

High temperature, especially when combined with high humidity, is far more troublesome. For heavy physical work, the maximum temperature at which efficiency is unimpared is about 80°F. At a temperature of 100°F most workers are performing at less than 50% efficiency. Efficiency approaches 0% when the temperature exceeds 110°F. Furthermore there is a substantial effect of heat stress on mental performance, problem solving, and reaction time after several hours of exposure to temperatures greater than 90°F.

Thus the extremes of climate likely to be encountered in some frontier areas do pose a real problem for workplace safety. Both the strength and precision of motion so necessary for safe performance on the drilling floor are likely to be affected. Speed of decision and reaction time may be slower. Finally, under extreme conditions, worker effectiveness drops rapidly with time. Accident rates are likely to rise sharply toward the end of a work shift. Shorter shifts than the traditional 12 on/12 off may be required if workplace safety is to be assured. Several actions can be taken to minimize the effect of climatic extremes. It is neither feasible nor appropriate here to indicate the engineering specifications for the resolution of all climatic problems in the workplace, but, wherever possible, temperature extremes should be avoided by the use of barriers, shields, enclosures, heaters, air conditioners, etc. Drilling equipment and work procedures may well have to be modified to minimize the amount of dexterity needed for operation in cold climates or the amount of physical effort required in hot climates.

Where it is not possible to modify extreme environmental conditions to bring them into the range of normal human tolerance, it may be possible to manage the work force to achieve a reasonable degree of effectiveness in climatic extremes. Specific actions that may be taken are: (1) Selection of personnel who can tolerate the conditions by a tryout in a similar but less hazardous physical environment; (2) permitting workers to become gradually acclimatized before full effort is required; (3) establishing appropriate work and rest schedules to minimize the buildup of physical stress; (4) rotating personnel, preferably before significant performance deterioration occurs; (5) modifying work procedures to minimize requirements for continuous high level human performance; (6) development of procedures to assess the work performance and physical well-being of workers on a continuous basis to identify potential problems at an early stage.

TRANSPORTATION HAZARDS IN FRONTIER AREAS

Transportation hazards are not usually considered as a part of workplace safety but they contribute significantly to the overall casualty rate. A central concern is the interface between the transport vehicle and the rig or platform. While it can be shown that weather is a minor contributor to workplace safety on a day-to-day basis, it has a major influence on the safe landing or loading of personnel or equipment from a boat or helicopter. In the North Sea, for example, severe weather conditions interferred with drilling operations only 10% of the time but interferred with transportation 26% of the time. In 1981, helicopters dominated personnel transport in the North Sea whereas helicopters shared the load of personnel transport with crewboats in the Gulf of Mexico. In the North Sea helicopter transportation accidents have represented the biggest single source of fatalities, accounting for 41.6% of all deaths in the Norwegian sector. Transportation accidents have also been a major source of casualties in the Gulf of Mexico, but in the Gulf the problem has been primarily one of the transition between the vehicle and the rig. In the experience of one major outer continental shelf operator, transportation accidents exceeded accidents from all other sources, with the exception of those occurring on the drill floor. Most of these accidents were the result of transferring personnel or equipment to and from boats during adverse conditions. Very few occurred in transit.

Because of the work cycle favored in the outer continental shelf, nearly the entire work-force makes a round trip shoreside monthly. Crewboat operators have been known to sail in gale force conditions, thus the exposure to the transportation interface hazard is quite high. Similarly, the heave and pitch of workboats and supply boats makes loading or unloading equipment in bad weather a risky business. Several fatalities were reported arising directly from unloading operations in bad weather. As drilling sites move farther from shore, the transportation problem is bound to get more difficult. The concept of the floatel, a rebuilt platform with full hotel services, merely shifts the problem from a smaller number of long trips to a greater number of short trips. Increasing the length of the work tour, keeping workers on the rig longer to minimize the number of shoreside trips, trades an increase in problems of motivation for a decrease in transportation risks. A partial solution to this problem may lie in the selection of workers who are willing to tolerate longer work tours for increased personal benefits.

WORKER CHARACTERISTICS

The problem of workplace accidents is, to a considerable extent, a problem of human characteristics, limitations, and attitudes. In the real world there are few working environments so benign that a poorly trained, incompetent, or careless person cannot come to harm, or harm those around him. Most analyses of the causes of workplace accidents show the individual worker as playing a major role, whether by performing an unsafe act, tolerating unsafe conditions, or failing to follow proper operating procedures.

Although not conclusive, the analysis of outer continental shelf drilling injuries tends to show that the rate of injury tends to decline with increasing experience on the job. One study showed that approximately three quarters of all injuries occurred to employees with less than one year on the job, and half of all injuries occurred during the first six months. The relationship between experience and injury rate cannot be expressed more definitively because no industrywide repository of employee records exists. Employment and safety records are maintained on a company by company basis, and there is no way of identifying the amount of experience or the number of accidents that a given worker had prior to that accumulated with this present employer. Further, the two job categories that suffer the most injuries and fatalities are roustabouts and roughnecks. In an industry growing as fast as offshore gas and oil drilling, most incumbents in these positions are likely to have only minimal experience.

Roustabouts and roughnecks arrive on the rig without skills and are taught on the job. Turnover rate at entry level is extremely high because many find the hard work and long hours unacceptable. These are also the people who work in teams of two to four to handly heavy loads. In such work, teamwork is essential to the safety of people and equipment, yet teamwork is a learned skill. Most of the accidents on the drill floor can be attributed to the failure of an individual to coordinate his work with that of others. The ability to fit into the work flow is based on a combination of physical skills, training, and attitudinal factors. Sensory perception, particularly vision, has a major relationship to accident likelihood. Physical strength, size, alertness, tolerance to stresses of work and exposure, and overall condition all influence the ability to avoid or avert dangerous situations.

The training of personnel in proper work procedures, and specifically in safety related concepts, can be particularly effective in reducing workplace accidents. Operators with effective in-house entry level training programs have a lower accident rate. But perhaps the most important human factor in accident causation is the attitude of the individual worker toward safety. His level of risk taking, his appraisal of hazardous situations, the margin of error he allows in the performance of his work, the level of vigilance he maintains, and finally his overall personality contribute to his likelihood of being involved in an accident.

Physical capability, training, experience, and attitudinal factors interact with the stresses of the environment, including noise, temperature, vibration, boredom, danger, and fatigue to result in less than optimum performance of assigned tasks. When sufficient deterioration occurs in the presence of a potentially dangerous situation, an accident occurs.

Workers willing to work in frontier areas may have qualitatively different attitudes toward safety and risk-taking than those willing to work in the more established areas. Frontier areas are physically more stressful in being geographically remote and presenting risks of an unknown nature. Work on the frontier may represent an adventure while work in the Gulf of Mexico may merely represent a job. The combination of relative isolation, physical stress, and novelty attracts individualists with a lessened regard for personal safety and a high tolerance for risk. In combination with the very real hazards imposed by the environment, workers with these characteristics may reduce workplace safety.

The expected increase in the rate of accidents in frontier areas may be several years away because operators drilling in frontier areas have been able to staff their rigs with a select group of experienced workers. This has been possible because frontier areas currently employ less than 10% of the U.S. offshore industry work force. As the demand for experienced workers rises because of increased drilling activities worldwide, the experienced labor force will be stretched thin and steps must be taken to maintain and improve current standards of workplace safety.

IMPROVING WORKPLACE SAFETY

There are three approaches to improving workplace safety. The first is the safety engineering approach. It is simple, direct, and intuitively obvious. It involves modifying the equipment or the workplace to eliminate the hazardous condition or the injury-producing agent common to a large number of accidents. Thus, if falls represent a major source of injury, then their frequency can be reduced by providing guard rails, or their effects can be attenuated by the use of nets or safety harnesses. The safety engineering approach is institutionalized in safety regulations that prescribe the design or the construction of specific equipments or safety devices.

The safety engineering approach usually results in a reduction of work related injuries to about 50% of their previous value. The plateau is reached when safety devices begin to be perceived as impediments to efficient operations in the workplace. Thus, workers in industrial plants frequently remove the safety interlocks prescribed by the Occupational Safety and Health Administration in order to perform their work more easily. When the author visited a drilling platform in 1981, he observed a worker climb on top of a guard rail on the upper deck, hook a leg around a post, and lean out over a 100 ft drop to free a jammed block on a crane. Perhaps this point of diminishing returns has not yet been reached on most drilling rigs, but the safety engineering approach may be at a point of marginal return.

The second approach to reduction of workplace involves *screening and selection of personnel.* Although the concept of "accident proneness" has lost favor in recent years, it is a fact that some workers simply have more accidents than others. The Marine Index Bureau has been collecting accident records of seamen for nearly half a century and can verify that in a working lifetime, some men have over ten times the number of accidents as others for the same degree of risk exposure. While plain bad luck may be the major factor for some of these men, it is probable that for many of the others there exists some combination of physical characteristics, personality, and attitude which makes accidents more likely. Indentification of these individuals can help reduce workplace accidents by (1) excluding them from potentially hazardous job situations; or (2) retraining them to exhibit safer patterns of behavior in dangerous situations.

In both instances it will be necessary to maintain safety records of offshore personnel independent of their work for a given employer. Without such records the individuals cannot be identified nor can a new employer be apprised of their accident likely behavior. Based on contemporary maritime and industrial experience, this approach is likely to be the most cost effective in the long run. It does require, however, an unprecedented degree of mutual cooperation in the drilling industry in the pooling of personnel illness and injury records and the sharing of safety information. Further, it requires a management educated to the realization that, even in a period of chronic labor shortage, it is often wise to reject a job applicant if he shows evidence of a poor safety record or is otherwise likely to be a poor performer.

The third approach to the reduction of workplace accidents has been termed the *motivational approach.* It suggests that the worker must be motivated to behave safely and that he must perceive the rationale behind the prudent behavior in the workplace. Common sense would suggest that protection of life and limb would be suffecient reason for workers to behave safely, but this is not the case. The survival motive is not as strong as it could be, since workers engage in unsafe behavior every day, but seldom have accidents. In addition, safe behavior often requires a greater expenditure of energy than a more expedient method of working. To combat this tendency, the motivational approach to safety tries to change workers preferences for, and satisfactions with, safe behavior.

This approach tries to get workers to identify unsafe behaviors and to suggest their own safer solutions. Safety is put on a competitive basis and rewards, immediate and direct, are offered for accident free periods. Feedback and reinforcement are offered whenever possible to encourage safety. The technique is effective and positive, but very fragile. It requires almost constant attention from supervisors. The accident rate rises to earlier levels shortly after this attention lapses.

The most important gap in our understanding and use of the motivational approach to workplace safety is the lack of attention to the concept of deliberate acceptance of danger or risk. Success stories throughout history have frequently defined people in terms of "courage," placing a high premium on taking chances. These themes are instilled in children and manifest themselves in adult behavior. A "heroic" individual may take a benign view of the dangers inherent in a given situation. The oil industry is particularly prone to the glorification of chance takers and wildcatters and proudly proclaims the risky nature of the business. It is not surprising, therefore, that the oil drilling community finds it difficult to establish freedom from accidents as a reasonable goal. Acceptance of risk is so ingrained in the industry psyche that it has become institutionalized as a way of life. The typical worker on an oil rig makes two bets with regard to risk: "If danger comes, I can handle it," and "I am betting that danger has a low probability."

Chance taking is a basic to American life. Personnel who volunteer to work in frontier areas subscribe, more than most, to this practice. A safety education and accident prevention program designed to combat dangerous risks requires the mobilization of personal, organizational, and peer group pressures. Company objectives are seldom the objectives of the individual worker; therefore, safety objectives must be defined to give sufficient positive incentive to the worker in terms of promotions and rewards to overcome any propensity for imprudent risk taking.

In summary, personnel problems in frontier areas are simply extensions of those already encountered on the outer continental shelf. The workplace itself represents no unusual hazards. Problems of the severe climatic environment can be controlled by proper selection of personnel and management of work procedures. It is likely that persons willing to work in frontier areas will be less stable and greater risk takers than those working in more mature regions. This implies that the accident rate may well increase unless the operators establish a strong commitment to workplace safety.

There is no single ideal way to enhance workplace safety offshore. Safety engineering is effective, particularly where a specific hazard can be clearly defined; however, it is eventually self-limiting when the precautionary measures interfere with normal work procedures. The personnel selection approach requires the institution of an independent record keeping agency and an effort to identify accident likely individuals. The motivational approach requires high-level commitment and constant attention on the part of supervisory and management personnel. The approaches to workplace safety are neither exclusive nor exhaustive and a combination of all may prove most effective.

NOTES TO CHAPTER 8

1. *Safety and Offshore Oil,* Committee on Assessment of OCS Activities, Marine Board, Assembly of Engineering, National Research Council, National Academy Press, Washington, D.C., 1981.
2. *Offshore Safety,* UK Department of Energy, London, Cmmd. 7841, March 1980.

3. *Risk Assessment: A Study of Risk Assessment Levels within Norwegian Off-shore Petroleum Activities,* The Royal Norwegian Council for Scientific and Industrial Research, Report No. 25-27/2, Nov. 1979.
4. *Safety Problems in the Offshore Petroleum Industry,* International Labor Organization, Geneva, 1978.
5. Snider, W.D., Buffleben, G.J., Harrald, J.R., Bishop, K.F., and Card, J.C., Management of Mid-Atlantic Offshore Development Risks, *Marine Technology,* Vol. 14, Oct. 1977, pp. 331-350.
6. McCormick, E.J., *Human Factors Engineering,* McGraw-Hill, New York, 1970.

Chapter 9
U.S. Geological Survey Regulatory Program for the Outer Continental Shelf

Thomas G. McCloskey

In 1970, the United States imported 21 percent of its oil supplies at a cost of $3 billion. Ten years later, imports accounted for 42 percent of the nation's oil supplies and the national bill for imports rose to a staggering $80 billion. During the same decade, domestic oil production steadily declined. These two interrelated trends, coupled with America's continued reliance on oil to satisfy nearly half of its energy needs, combined to confound policy makers, undermine the nation's economy, and jeopardize the country's national security.

The Reagan Administration has pledged to reverse these trends, emphasizing production, rather than conservation. It is also clear that the Administration intends to open up unprecedented amounts of public lands, particularly on the Outer Continental Shelf (OCS), to energy resource exploration and development activities.

U.S. OFFSHORE LEASING POLICY

Up to 1982, only 2.5 percent of the OCS had been leased and this area has been the source of approximately nine percent of the nation's domestic oil production and about 22 percent of its domestic gas production. These figures are not reflective, however, of the vast potential of the shelf. Experts estimate that from 30 to 60 percent of the nation's undiscovered oil and gas resources may be contained in OCS lands.

Consistent with Reagan Administration policy, the Secretary of the Department of the Interior in 1982 announced plans to increase dramatically petroleum industry access to the nation's estimated one billion acres of OCS lands. These plans were embodied in a proposed revision to the Five-Year Leasing Schedule, which would make 300 million acres available annually until 1985. Sales would emphasize initial and repeat leases in "frontier" areas, and broaden sale areas to include whole OCS regions.

If the proposed schedule were adopted and adhered to, there would be an unprecedented level of activity on the OCS in the years ahead. The proposed schedule would, in effect, open a new era for offshore energy operations, an era not without peril to the nation's marine, coastal, and human environments. Much of the unleased acreage with the highest resource potential is located in environmentally sensitive areas. Calls for the accelerated leasing of OCS lands are not new, nor is opposition to these calls on environmental grounds. Indeed, there are many individuals who question whether the federal OCS gas and oil program is adequate to protect the environment at current, let alone projected levels of leasing.

With the prospect of accelerated leasing, it is both timely and appropriate to examine the adequacy of environmental protection measures currently applied to OCS energy activities. Such an examination involves the description and evaluation of the pollution control and environmental protection provisions in the regulatory program administered by the U.S. Geological Survey (USGS), which is the federal agency with primary responsibility for the regulation of OCS gas and oil operations.

U.S. GEOLOGICAL SURVEY AND THE OCS LANDS ACT

In determining the adequacy of the environmental protection measures currently contained in the USGS's regulations, it is important to investigate the origins of these measures and to understand the nature of the concerns that led to the adoption of these measures. The federal OCS gas and oil program was established in 1953 with the passage of the Submerged Lands Act, which established federal government jurisdiction over OCS lands, and the OCS Lands Act, which created a mechanism for the leasing and management of these lands. From the outset, the USGS has had responsibility for developing, administering, and enforcing a program to insure, among other things, that OCS gas and oil operations were conducted in an environmentally sound fashion. During the first sixteen years of the program, however, very little emphasis was placed on pollution control and environmental protection measures.

This attitude changed in January 1969 when a blowout at a production platform in the Santa Barbara Channel resulted in a spill estimated at 33,000 barrels of oil that coated miles of prime beach with oily tar, killed thousands of seabirds, and raised the specter of far reaching, short- and long-term disruptions of the area's marine environment. Although this was the first significant oil spill on the OCS, the incident focused nationwide attention on the potential environmental impacts of OCS oil and gas development.

Within eight months of the spill, the USGS published revised regulations specifically designed to strengthen the pollution control requirements applied to OCS operations. However, this action did not quiet program critics who saw the subsequent blowouts and oil spills in the Gulf of Mexico (in 1970 and 1971) as further evidence of fundamental deficiencies in the program. Political pressure began to mount for a more comprehensive and fundamental revision of the USGS's program.

Calls for change were fueled, in part, by the emergence of the environmental movement in the early 1970s. The Santa Barbara Channel oil spill served as a catalyst for a general upsurge in public awareness and concern about the impact of man's activities on the environment. Within a year of the spill, Congress enacted the National Environmental Policy Act (NEPA), ushering in an era of major environmental statutes focusing on the marine environment. In addition to NEPA, the following acts addressed environmental policy:

- Federal Water Pollution Control Act of 1972 and Amendments of 1976
- Coastal Zone Management Act of 1972 and Amendments of 1976
- Marine Protection, Research, and Sanctuaries Act of 1972
- Marine Mammal Protection Act of 1972
- Endangered Species Act of 1973

Most of these acts had little direct effect on the USGS's program. They did tend, however, to accentuate the program's lack of specificity in terms of pollution control and environmental protection requirements and standards. Moreover, they increased the overall complexity of the federal OCS gas and oil program and, for the first time, provided other federal agencies with more environmentally-oriented missions, providing mechanisms for greater involvement in the review and evaluation of OCS oil and gas activities.

AMENDMENTS TO THE OCS LANDS ACT

As criticism of the Survey's oil and gas program continued to mount, efforts surfaced to amend the OCS Lands Act of 1953. This Act was viewed as hopelessly outmoded and seriously deficient, particularly in terms of provisions designed to protect the environment. Legislation to amend this statute was introduced in the U.S. Senate (S 3221) in March 1974 in the hopes of stimulating OCS energy resource development activities by addressing, in a comprehensive fashion, criticism directed toward the federal OCS gas and oil program.

In energy messages of 1973 and 1974, the Nixon Administration had unveiled plans to more than treble (from three to ten million acres) the amount of OCS lands to be leased each year. The Administration viewed increased access to these lands as a viable way to reduce the nation's dependence on uncertain and increasingly expensive foreign supplies of oil. On the other hand, most coastal states, the environmental community, and others viewed the proposal as an unprecedented threat to the nation's marine, coastal, and human environments, and made it clear that their support for *any* increase in OCS leasing was contingent on the passage of the amendments under consideration by Congress.

Despite ever increasing support for the amendments, proponents of change were unable to overcome the opposition of the Nixon Administration and the succeeding Ford Administration. However, the Carter Administration, which took office in January 1977, announced its support of efforts to amend the OCS Lands Act of 1953. Following sixteen months of intense debate in both the Senate and the House of Representatives, and three months of work by a conference committee, a complex package of amendments was overwhelmingly approved by Congress and signed into law by President Carter in September 1978.

In the Amendments, the need to protect the environment was put on an equal footing with the need to develop OCS energy resources. This is reflected in Section 102(2) of the Amendments, which states that one of the purposes of the Amendments is to "preserve, protect, and develop oil and natural gas resources in the Outer Continental Shelf in a manner which is consistent with the need . . . to balance orderly energy resource development with protection of the human, marine, and coastal environments." This "balancing" criterion is integrated into every aspect of the OCS gas and oil leasing (see Section 18), exploration (see Section 11), and development and production (see Section 25) processes, and given teeth in Section 5(a) (1) (B) of the Amendments which prohibits the Secretary of Interior from approving or allowing to continue an activity which poses ". . . a threat of serious, irreparable, or immediate harm or damage to the marine, coastal, or human environments." The scope and complexity of the Secretary's responsibility under these provisions is reflected in the following definitions of "marine environment," "coastal environment," and "human environment" contained in Section 201 of the Amendments:

(g) The term 'marine environment' means the physical, atmospheric, and biological components, conditions, and factors which interactively determine the productivity, state, condition, and quality of the marine ecosystem, including the waters of the high seas, the contiguous zone, transitional and intertidal areas, salt marches, and wetlands within the coastal zone and on the Outer Continental Shelf;

(h) The 'coastal environment' means the physical, atmospheric, and biological components, conditions, and factors which interactively determine the productivity, state, condition, and quality of the terrestrial ecosystem from the shoreline inward to the boundaries of the coastal zone;

(i) The term 'human environment' means the physical, social and economic components, conditions, and factors which interactively determine the state, condition, and quality of living conditions, employment, and health of those affected, directly or indirectly, by activities occurring on the Outer Continental Shelf. . .

In short, the OCS Lands Act Amendments of 1978 substantially strengthened and clarified the nation's commitment to protect the environment while endorsing efforts to expedite the exploration and development of OCS energy resources. The Amendments created some new environmental protection measures and established a more specific legal underpinning for many of the existing environmental protection measures in the USFS's OCS gas and oil program.

Most of these measures were specifically designed to address the two principal environmental issues that emerged from 1969 to 1976. First, the Santa Barbara Channel oil spill in 1969 gave rise to concerns over the potential for and impact of major oil spills, and, second, the calls for accelerated leasing of OCS lands in the 1970s had generated concerns over the general environmental, social, and economic impacts of OCS energy activities, particularly in frontier areas.

During the 1970s, concerns over oil spills from blowouts, pipeline leaks and failures, and tanker collisions heightened as OCS energy activities moved progressively into deep-water areas and more hazardous and hostile operating environments. It was a concern based upon perceived limitations of existing technology and human performance, and the fact that spilled oil can cause short-term lethal, sublethal, and habitat alteration effects on benthic and pelagic organisms and marine mammals and seabirds. Also, spilled oil can foul commercial and recreational fishing grounds, coastal facilities, and beaches, resulting in large economic losses. Compounding concerns over the fate and effect of spilled oil are doubts about industry or government ability to contain and clean up spills, particularly in rough seas and Arctic ice conditions.

With the push in the mid- and late 1970s for the accelerated leasing of OCS lands, questions also arose over the primary and secondary environmental, social, and economic impacts of OCS energy development activities. Although most of the nation's coastal areas are heavily populated and developed, large stretches of the coastline are undeveloped (particularly in Alaska and central and northern California), and relatively few coastal areas have had any experience with OCS gas and oil operations and their allied onshore support facilities. Doubts continue to be expressed over the capacity of these areas to accommodate OCS energy development activities without adversely impacting the environment, altering existing lifestyles, or interfering with other, potentially conflicting, uses of these areas.

U.S. GEOLOGICAL SURVEY REGULATIONS

To a degree, these two issues have played a role in the development of the USGS's OCS and gas and oil regulatory program since its inception. However, events in the late 1960s and early 1970s clearly pushed them to the forefront of the USGS's considerations, and they were reflected in the system of regulations and regulatory directives the USGS developed to govern exploration, development, and production operations on the OCS.

The regulations appear in Title 30 of the Code of Federal Regulations, and the regulatory directives take the form OCS Orders and Notices to Lessees and Operators. The pollution control and environmental protection measures that pertain to leasehold drilling and production operations are mandated under the provisions of Part 250 of Title 30. Under §250.30(b) of the regulations, lessees are required to ". . . conduct operations on a lease in a manner that does not . . . threaten or damage . . . the marine, coastal, or human environments." Furthermore, under §250.43(a) (1) and §250.57 of the regulations, lessees are prohibited from polluting land, water, or air resources. Protection of the environment is to be achieved through the performance of all operations in a safe and workmanlike manner (see §250.46) and, when necessary and practicable, the application of the best available and safest technologies (see §250.30(c)).

Before commencing any operations on an OCS lease, a lessee must demonstrate that the proposed operations comply with the general provisions outlined above. For example, before a lessee can initiate exploratory drilling operations the lessee must prepare, submit, and obtain approval of an Exploration Plan (see §250.34-1) and an Application for a Permit to Drill (see §250.36). Also, in most OCS areas, the Exploration Plan must be accompanied by a detailed Environmental Report (see §250.34-3(a)).

Continuing with this example, information on the measures the lessee will employ and the procedures the lessee will follow to prevent an oil spill must be presented in the Exploration Plan and Application for a Permit to Drill. Under §250.34-1(a) (1) (ii) and §250.36(b) (1) of the regulations, the lessee is required to submit information on the pollution prevention and control features of the drilling apparatus, including a detailed description of the lessee's casing, cementing, mud, and blowout prevention programs.

Under §250.41(a) (1) of the regulations, the lessee is required to ". . . take all necessary precautions to keep its wells under control at all times." Under §250.41(a) (2) through (4) of the regulations and OCS Order No. 2 very detailed requirements and standards are specified for exploratory drilling operations. First, the lessee must ". . . case and cement all wells with a sufficient number of strings of casing . . . to: prevent release of fluids from any stratum through the well bore (directly or indirectly) into the sea; prevent communication between separate hydrocarbon-bearing strata . . . and between hydrocarbon- and water-bearing strata; protect freshwater strata from contamination; support unconsolidated sediments; and otherwise provide a means of control of the formation pressures the fluids (see §250.41(a)(2))." The casing must be strong enough to withstand collapse, bursting, tensile, and other stresses, and the cement must be strong enough to anchor and support the casing. OCS Order No. 2 specifies the type and normal installation sequence of the casing strings, depths at which each string must be set, cementing procedures, and pressure-testing standards for the casing.

Second, under §250.41(a)(3) of the regulations, the lessee must ". . . maintain, readily accessible for use, quantities of drilling mud sufficient to assure well control." OCS Order No. 2 requires lessees to stockpile or have ready access to sufficient quantities of mud to maintain well control under normal and emergency situations. Order No. 2 also specifies the type of mud-system monitoring equipment that must be installed, standards for mud tests, and how the mud is to be used during drilling operations.

Finally, the USGS's regulations require the lessee to ". . . install, use, and test blowout preventers and related well-control equipment in a manner necessary to prevent blowouts (see §250.41(a)(4) and (5))." OCS Order No. 2 describes, in great detail, the type, capabilities, and sequence of equipment that must be on surface and subsea blowout preventers. Furthermore, the Order specifies specific standards for this equipment, and the frequency with which it must be inspected and tested during the course of drilling operations.

It should be noted that the requirements discussed above also apply to drilling activities during the development stage of OCS operations (see §250.34-2(a)(1)(ii)). At the development stage lessees are also required to install and maintain, under OCS Order No. 5, subsurface-safety valves on all production wells as a further safeguard against an oil spill.

One of the most important accident prevention features in the USGS's regulatory program is the requirement that "(t)he lessee . . .

utilize personnel who are trained and competent to drill and operate wells (see §250.41(a)(1))." The USGS has developed a standard training program on well-control equipment and techniques for drilling, and OCS Order No. 2 requires each person engaged in drilling operations to successfully complete a USGS-approved basic well-control course every four years and a refresher course annually. This training requirement is an important factor in insuring that OCS gas and oil drilling operations are conducted in the safest manner possible thereby reducing the threat of an oil spill.

Despite the measures discussed above, there is still the chance that an oil spill might occur, and the USGS's regulations require the lessee to be fully prepared to handle all oil spill incidents. Under §250.34-1(a) (ii) and 2(a) (ii) of the regulations and OCS Order No. 7, the lessee is required to prepare and submit an oil spill contingency plan which describes all of the equipment, materials, and supplies available on site, locally, and regionally to contain and cleanup an oil spill. It must specify the amount of time it will take to deploy and activate the containment and cleanup of equipment, and provide for varying degrees of response activities depending upon the severity of the spill. The plan must also contain information on the notification procedures the lessee will follow to assure the prompt reporting of a spill to federal, state, and local regulatory agencies.

ENVIRONMENTAL REPORTS

The aforementioned provisions are designed, among other things to prevent oil spills and to minimize their impact if they occur. Information on the potential environmental impact of an oil spill is provided in a separate document — the Environment Report. Except in the western Gulf of Mexico, Environmental Reports must be submitted with all plans of exploration and plans of development (see §250.34-1(a) (2) (i) and -2(a) (3) (i)).

The Environmental Report must also contain other information that is used by numerous federal, state, and local governmental agencies and the public to assess the primary and secondary environmental, social, and economic impacts of proposed OCS activities. The regulatory provisions that cover the prescribed contents of an Environmental Report are contained in §250.34-3 of the regulations and OCS Order No. 7.

Also, the USGS has published guidelines, in the form of a Notice to Lessees and Operators, to assist lessees in the preparation of these documents.

Essentially, there are three sections in an Environmental Report. In the first section, the lessee must describe the proposed action. In the second, the lessee must describe the environmental setting in which the proposed action will take place and, in the third section, the lessee must describe the actual or potential impacts of the proposed action on the environment.

The first section must contain a brief summary of the nature and scope of the activities described in the accompanying plan of exploration or plan of development. The type of facility to be used and the location, timing, and sequence of the proposed activities must be fully described. Information must be provided on the number of people that will be engaged in the activities; the type, amount, and origin of the supplies to be used; and the proposed travel modes and routes for moving personnel and supplies to and from the site of the proposed activities, and the frequency of such trips. The location and type of all onshore support facilities must also be described.

The first section of the Environmental Report must also contain a summary of the information contained in the oil spill contingency plan, as well as a discussion of the quantity, composition, duration, rates of discharge, and ultimate disposition of solid, liquid, and gaseous wastes and pollutants likely to be generated by project-related offshore and onshore activities. Finally, this section must detail how the lessee plans to comply with federal and state requirements, avoid conflicts with nearly pending actions, and monitor operations to insure that they are conducted in an environmentally sound fashion.

In the second section of the report, the lessee must describe environmental features that may affect or be affected by the proposed activities. The following parameters must be considered: geology, meteorology, physical oceanography, other uses of the area, flora and fauna, and socioeconomics. The lessee must conduct site-specific surveys to collect geologic information, and, in some areas, surveys are also required to gather site-specific cultural resource and biological information.

Information gathered in the first two sections must be synthesized in the third to determine the direct, indirect, and cumulative effects

of the proposed activities on the marine, coastal, and human environments. It is in this section, for example, that the impacts of an oil spill
must be evaluated. Once the actual or potential effects are determined,
the lessee must discuss alternatives to the proposed activities which
would result in less risk to the environment, and fully describe all unavoidable adverse environmental effects.

The information contained in an Environmental Report is used by
the USGS to prepare an Environmental Assessment. Environmental
Assessments, in turn, are used to determine whether the proposed activities constitute a major federal action requiring the preparation of an
Environmental Impact Statement (EIS). If the USGS determines that
an EIS is required, then the proposed activities are subject to additional, much more exhaustive, analysis. Also, an Environmental Report is
used by coastal states with approved coastal management programs to
determine whether the proposed activities are consistent with state or
local coastal management programs.

Once activities are approved by the USGS and commence on the
OCS, lessees are required to comply, under §250.30(a) of the regulations, with the provisions of all applicable laws, regulations, OCS Orders, the terms of the lease, and other written or oral orders issued by
the USGS. The USGS enforces the pollution control and environmental protection measures applicable to OCS operations through a variety
of mechanisms. First, lessees are required to maintain detailed well
records and submit them upon demand to the USGS (see §250.38).
Second, lessees are required to report all oil spills or the leakage of
oil or waste to the marine environment to the USGS, and lessees are
responsible for the control and total removal of these substances
(see §250.43(a) (3) and (B) (1), (3)). Third, under §250.34-1(j) (1)
and §250.34-2(1) (1) the USGS must periodically review activities
being conducted under approved plans of exploration or plans of development to determine whether changes in information or detectable
problems require revisions in the plans or operations. Fourth, under
§250.11(a) (3) and (4) the USGS conducts periodic onsite inspections
of OCS facilities. During these inspections, all environmental protection and safety equipment designed to prevent or ameliorate blowouts,
fires, spillages or other major accidents are carefully examined. Finally, under §250.12(a) (1) (ii) of the regulations, the USGS has the au-
thority to suspend or temporarily prohibit any activity that threatens

". . . serious, irreparable, or immediate harm or damage . . . to the marine, coastal, or human environments."

CONCLUSION

In summary, the USGS's regulatory program requires lessees to protect the marine, coastal, and human environments and prohibits lessees from polluting land, water, or air resources. To insure compliance with these general requirements, USGS regulations and OCS Orders contain specific provisions designed to prevent oil spills and provide government agencies and the public information on the primary and secondary environmental, social, and economic effects of OCS drilling and production activities. Moreover, the USGS has a variety of mechanisms at its disposal to monitor operations and to act decisively when OCS oil and gas activities threaten the environment.

The current USGS program is the product of years of painstaking work, work designed to build a consensus behind OCS gas and oil activities by addressing, in a forthright fashion, legitimate concerns that have been expressed over the actual or potential environmental impacts of these activities. The USGS has responded well to the criticisms that have been leveled against its program. It has developed not only a comprehensive program, but an effective one.

The true effectiveness of the program is reflected in two facts. First, there has not been a major oil spill on the OCS since 1971. Even the program's harshest critics admit that the record during the past ten years has been quite good. Second, the vast majority of coastal states now accept OCS energy resource development as an important and necessary part of the nation's energy program. This contrasts sharply with the widespread coastal state opposition to OCS oil and gas activities that existed in the mid-1970s. This shift in attitude can be attributed, in part, to adjustments made in the USGS program. In the 1980s the coastal states are playing a more important role in the OCS decision making process, and they receive the type of information they need, when they need it, to plan for and accommodate offshore energy activities.

If the Reagan Administration wants to achieve its ambitious OCS leasing goals, it must recognize the events and forces that have helped shape the USGS's program, and the efforts, over the past decade, to develop a program that coastal states, the leaders of environmental interest groups, and the public knows, understands, and have confidence in. The existing USGS program is not perfect. Further refinements and improvements may be necessary. However, the evidence indicates that the program is fundamentally sound and, most importantly, that it works.

Chapter 10
Environmental Effects of Offshore Drilling

Dale Straughan

Since the 1960s, there has been an increasing awareness of the less obvious and more subtle long-term impacts of mans influence on the natural environment. More and more attention has been paid to the environmental effects of offshore drilling. This has included large scale field studies in potential lease areas funded by the Bureau of Land Management (BLM); extensive field studies in the Gulf of Mexico, where oil production in the marine environment has been under way for many years, such as petroleum industry funded Gulf Universities Research Consortium (GURC) studies; smaller studies to define changes during operations at specific oil producing platforms, such as the American Petroleum Institute (API) study in the Santa Barbara Channel; and longer term, before and after studies at oil rigs in the North Sea by the Oil Pollution Research Unit.

In addition, there have been studies that have concentrated on specific aspects of offshore oil and gas operation: for example, the effects of drilling muds, bioaccumulation of petroleum in tissues, response of organisms to low levels of pollutants from petroleum operations. In fact, on the surface it looks as though all the pieces of the jigsaw puzzle are there. All that needs to be done is put these pieces together to define the environmental effects of offshore drilling.

Before we begin this process, let us define what we are trying to do. Are we trying to present a description of observed changes in areas of offshore gas and oil operations? Are we trying to define which changes are due to the oil and gas operations and which are due to other factors? Are we trying to define which is a significant change due to gas and oil operations? Are we trying to define which of these significant changes is detrimental and what should be done about it?

All of these questions need to be answered on a scientific basis before the information is in the form in which it can be used in the decision making and management process. Unfortunately, in the past, personal values have entered into the system too early. Both personal and political values will enter into the decision making and management process, but sound scientific information should be an essential part of the process. This information can be obtained by a variety of methods, and a review of the literature shows that good use of many methods has been made in different programs. However, this has resulted in a patchy emergence of the data. Many of the pieces in the jigsaw are still missing while in other instances the information is there but the pieces will not fit together.

In general there are two large problems associated with providing a sound scientific basis for the decision and management process that have been neglected: first, the natural variability in time and space; and, second, an inadequate definition of significant changes. The natural variability in time and space is not a new phenomenon, so it is surprising that it is ignored frequently.

NATURAL VARIABILITY IN TIME AND SPACE

Some interesting examples of changes have been recorded during the last ten years. For example, analyses of the sea surface data for the Southern California Bight showed that there was an overall 4°C average difference in water temperatures between winter 1975-1976 and winter 1976-1977, as shown in Figure 10-1. There was an onset of warm winter waters, decreased upwelling, and extremely clear water at the end of 1976 in Santa Monica Bay.[1] Changing oceanographic conditions were recorded not only in the Southern California Bight, but in late 1976 in the eastern North Pacific Ocean.[2] In other words there was a well documented, very widespread oceanographic change.

More localized and short-term changes can occur in the form of irregular pulses of either warm or cold water. In July 1977, cold water "pulses" generally lasting three to four days were recorded in the San Onofre area of southern California, as shown in Figure 10-2.

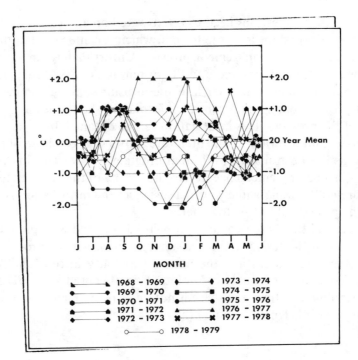

Figure 10-1. Sea Surface Temperature Deviation in Southern California Bight, 1968-1979.

Note that all three pulses were not recorded throughout the water column.

It is predicted that such oceanographic variations will cause changes in the biota in the area. One review of ocean variability and its biological effects discussed the relationship of the distribution of a number of pelagic and planktonic species to changing oceanic conditions.[3] The types of relationships are frequently difficult to detect because of a long lag phase between cause and effect. For example, in central California, unusually high ocean temperature during the egg brooding period of the dungeness crab (*Cancer magister*) in 1957 preceded the decline in landings by three years, and those landings remained low as ocean temperatures, on the average, remaind relatively high.[4] A similar relationship also exists between ocean temperature and fluctuation in crab landings in northern California.

The response time of organisms to such natural variability will vary with the type of exposure of the organism. For example, a migratory

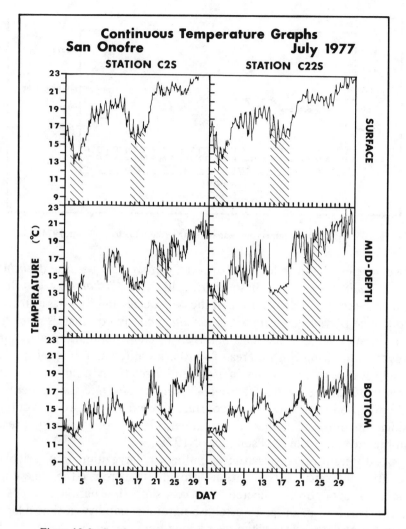

Figure 10-2. Continuous Temperature Graphs, San Onofre, July 1977.

fish such as the albacore, *Thunnus alalunga,* appears to respond rapidly
to ambient water temperature, food availability, and thermal gradients.
Thus, when the transition zone is distinct in the northern Pacific Ocean,
the migrating albacore are concentrated in this area, but when the transition zone is broad and indistinct, the fish are spread over a much wider
area of ocean.[5]

Population structure of sedentary species may also change in a relatively short time span if the species has a short life cycle. For example,

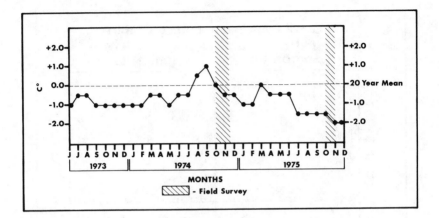

Figure 10-3. Sea Surface Temperature Variation in Southern California Bight, 1974 and 1975.

two species of the sedentary barnacle, *Chthamalus fissus* and *Chthamalus dalli,* are recorded in southern California. *Chthamalus fissus* has the more southern distribution of the two species and thus has a greater tolerance of warmer water. *Chthamalus dalli,* in contrast, is near the southern extreme of its range in this area. These populations were surveyed in the King Harbor area of southern California following a relatively warm water summer in 1974 and a relatively cold water summer in 1975, as shown in Figure 10-3. *Chthamalus fissus* was generally abundant on both surveys. In contrast, *C. dalli* was recorded in only a single quadrant after the warm summer of 1974, but was widespread in the area after the cold summer of 1975.[6]

As different organisms are responding to a large number of variables at different rates, extrapolation through time from either one data point, or data points collected over a very short time period, is impossible. Therefore in order to establish natural variability in time a large number of data points taken over a long time period are needed. This problem was noted after a reexamination of the Offshore Ecology Investigation (OEI) data: "The natural variability inherent in the biological, physical, and chemical processes in the Gulf of Mexico precludes acquisition of adequate, representative, or valid baseline data in a period limited to two years."[7] Ecological data are accumulating to suggest that the ideal may be seven to ten years for marine organisms.

Variability in space is also important. A study that accounts for natural variability through space can frequently reduce the time needed to study the different variability encountered through time. One obvious problem of variability in space was documented in studies after the *Metula* oil spill where levels of oil contamination were found to vary from 0 to 25% (CC14 extractables) in a quadrant with a 30 foot side.[8] Subtidal studies in natural oil seep areas at Coal Oil Point in southern California also showed significant variations in petroleum in the sediments in short distances.[9] Therefore, in order to determine the exposure of infaunal organisms to petroleum in sediments, the organisms as well as the sediments for petroleum analysis, must come from the same sample.[10]

The natural environment may also vary over short distances. For example, many beaches in southern California are composed of a series of cusps and hollows. Both abiotic and biotic data can differ significantly between the top of a well-developed cusp and the bottom of the adjacent hollow at the same intertidal level.

The examples presented of responses to natural change have been of pelagic or planktonic species or of those from intertidal areas. It is generally believed that there is less variability in the environment and in the biota as one moves into deeper water. However, the level of variability has generally been poorly defined. Studies of the abiotic parameters in 30 to 40 ft of water in southern California from 1974 through 1978 showed a significant change in bottom water temperature, dissolved oxygen, and salinity between summer 1976 and summer 1977.[11] Preliminary perusal of the companion biotic data revealed changes in space and time. Analysis of the biotic data are still in progress so that at the moment it is impossible to determine if these changes are significant.

INADEQUATE DEFINITION OF SIGNIFICANT CHANGE

What is a significant change? This can be determined statistically but normally requires the basis of a rigorous sampling regime. In the field, such a sampling regime requires replicate sampling at each sampling site or quadrant. Single point and line transect sampling programs are generally limited by their lack of establishment of natural variation in samples. Recent literature, in particular papers by W. Smith, have considered field sampling problems designed to obtain the least probable error with limited funding, with some knowledge of the area, and with no background knowledge of the area.[12] Such data may then be analyzed statistically and their mathematical significance determined.

However, mathematical significance does not necessarily imply biological, environmental, and/or health related significance. The mathematical significance tells us: (a) There is an important variation from the background data it was tested against, and (b) the variation was unlikely to occur by chance at a predetermined level of probability. An example may be a change in the composition of the benthic infauna following the disturbance of sediments during construction. Such a change could be measured and be statistically significant. However, since the sediments are reworked by ocean currents, the benthic infaunal population will change again so that it is within the natural variability recorded under similar conditions in the area. This would be considered a statistically significant impact of short-term duration but not of long-term biological, environmental, or health-related importance.

A double standard has developed that has resulted in more stringent environmental restrictions on water than on land or air. Most environmental restrictions for land or air are related to public health issues, with some consideration of endangered species and ecological reserves. The ocean, on the other hand, is frequently treated as one large ecological reserve in which no change is to be tolerated. Perhaps the case is somewhat overstated, but the result frequently is the dumping of waste created at sea on the land and at great expense. In general, there is no clear indication of the best medium — land, sea, or air — to deal with this waste material.

This leads to a basic problem of defining the level of change that the biota, the environment, and man cannot accommodate. Consider again the example of a statistically significant change that was judged to be not of biological, environmental, or health-related long-term importance. Repetition of such an event could lead to a consistent change in the infauna, but because it is a viable and productive community, this may again be considered unimportant in biological, environmental, and health-related terms. However, the reverse could occur. The repetitive changes could be so disruptive that the area could become generally depauperate. This may or may not be important by the present terms of reference, depending on the size of the area impacted in comparison to the size of a similar area unimpacted.

Definition of the environmental change that will be considered significant, and why, is generally lacking from most environmental studies.[13] It is just not enough to determine that there has been or will be a change, but the importance of this change must be defined and determined.

All this leads back to the jigsaw puzzle that will not fit together. Many of the comments regarding the smaller two-year study in the Gulf of Mexico apply to the total picture, even though the authors were optimistic that the BLM studies in the Gulf of Mexico when added to the OEI studies could sufficiently supplement the initial studies to eliminate many of the early problems.

While the scientific information in general appears patchy, some of these patches have provided valuable pieces of information. For example, as the data have accumulated, it appears that concern over the impact of drilling muds was much greater than their actual impact. In general, most data have substantiated a widely held belief that due to a greater dilution factor offshore than nearshore, the impacts of offshore drilling are less than those of nearshore drilling. In all instances, however, the products have been brought ashore for use, so that the environmental problems of transport onshore are similar whether the products come from offshore or nearshore operations.

All conclusions on this subject should be approached with caution. In most instances the impact of offshore operations have appeared less than the impact of nearshore operations. Yet long term before-and-after studies near oil rigs in the North Sea have revealed changes in the types, abundance, and diversity of species as far as 3,000 m from drilling rigs.[14] These studies have also showed an increase in opportunistic species in the area. The final question is, "Why did these changes occur in the North Sea and not in other areas studied?" or should the question be, "Why were these changes detected in the North Sea studies and not in other studies?"

NOTES TO CHAPTER 10

1. Mearns, A.J., "Changing Coastal Conditions: 1979 Compared to the Past 25 Years," *Southern California Water Research Project Report 1979-1980*, pp. 273-284.
2. Cayon, D.R., "Regimes and Events in Recent Climatic Variables," *CalCOFI Rep.*, Vol. *xxi*, 1980, pp. 90-101; Tont, S.A. and Delistraty, D.A., "The

Effects of Climate on Terrestrial and Marine Populations," *CalCOFI Rep.,* *Vol. xxi,* 1980, pp. 85-89.

3. Lasker, R., "Ocean Variability and Its Biological Effects — Regional Review — Northeast Pacific," *Rapp. P. -v. Reun. Cons. int. Explor. Mer.,* Vol. 173, 1978, pp. 168-181.

4. Wild, P.W., "Effects of Seawater Temperature on Spawning, Egg Development, Hatching Success, and Population Fluctuations of the Dungeness Crab, *Cancer magister,"* *CalCOFI Rep.,* Vol. xxi, 1980, pp. 115-120.

5. Laurs, R.M. and Lynn, R.J., "Seasonal Migration of Albacore, *Thunnus alalunga,* into North American Coastal Waters, Their Distribution, Relative Abundance and Associations with Transition Zone Waters," *Fish. Bull. U.S.,* Vol. 75, 1977, pp. 793-822.

6. Straughan, D., *Impact of Southern California Edison's Operations on Intertidal Solid Substrates in King Harbor,* Report to Southern California Edison, Rosemead, CA, 80-RD-95, 1980, 87 pp.

7. Bender, M.E., Reish, D.J., and Ward, C.H., "Re-examination of the Offshore Ecology Investigation." In: *The Offshore Ecology Investigation. Effects of Oil Drilling and Production in a Coastal Environment,* Rice University Studies, Vol. 65, 1979, pp. 35-118.

8. Straughan, D., "Biological Survey of Intertidal Areas in the Straits of Magellan in January, 1975, Five Months After the Metula Oil Spill," *Symposium on Fate and Effects of Petroleum Hydrocarbons in Marine Ecosystems and Organisms.* Seattle, Washington, November 1976, 1977, pp. 247-260.

9. Straughan, D., "Sublethal Effects of Natural Chronic Exposure to Petroleum in the Marine Environment," *American Petroleum Institute No. 4280,* 1976, 123 pp.

10. Bender, Reish, and Ward.

11. Straughan, D., *Benthic Physical and Chemical Stability in King Harbor 1974-1978,* Report to Southern California Edison, Rosemead, CA, 80-RD-113, 1980, 52 pp.

12. Smith, W., *Survey Design in Marine Environment: Three Examples,* National Technical Information Service PB80-199326, 1980, 16 pp.

13. Taxon, Inc., *Review and Evaluation of Benthic Environmental Studies at San Onofre Nuclear Generation Station,* Report to Southern California Edison, Rosemead, CA, 80-RD-127, 1980.

14. Addy, J.M., Levell, D., and Hartley, J.P., "Biological Monitoring of Sediments in the Ekofisk Oilfield." In: *Proc. Conference on Assessment of Ecological Impacts of Oil Spills sponsored by A.I.B.S.,* Keystone, Colorado, 1978, pp. 514-539.

Index

THE FUTURE OF GAS AND OIL FROM THE SEA

Edited by **Gerard J. Mangone**

Dwindling domestic supplies of gas and oil, and the continued threat of dependency on foreign sources have made it imperative to find new reserves. *The Future of Gas and Oil from the Sea* investigates the geological, engineering, and environmental aspects of offshore sources. It thoroughly examines the resources, strategies, and concepts involved, as well as the latest methods of exploration.

Based on a national conference held by the Center for the Study of Marine Policy at the University of Delaware, this manual offers the opinions of top energy professionals. It features vital information contributed by geologists, engineers, and production managers from the leading energy companies and U.S. government agencies.

Significant evidence is presented to show that as much gas and oil remains to be found under the world's oceans as has already been found under dry land. Technical problems related to tapping undersea reserves are covered in sections on drilling and recovering hydrocarbon resources from frontier areas, from under deep water roiled by high winds, and from frigid areas.

Numerous illustrations accompany information on the latest advances in drilling rigs and their equipment, new types of tankers and vessel transfers, and improvements in pipeline transmission of gas and oil. Fully explored is the crucial human factor in training and safety with regard to complex equipment. Also discussed are the effects of government regulation on the offshore industry. Special attention is given to the Outer Continental Shelf Act and its administration, as well as the problems of ascertaining the environmental effects of the recovery of gas and oil from the seabed.